Penguin Education

Story The first book
an anthology of stories and pictures
edited by David Jackson and Dennis Pepper

D1796348

Story
the first book
an anthology of stories and pictures
edited by
David Jackson and Dennis Pepper

Penguin Books

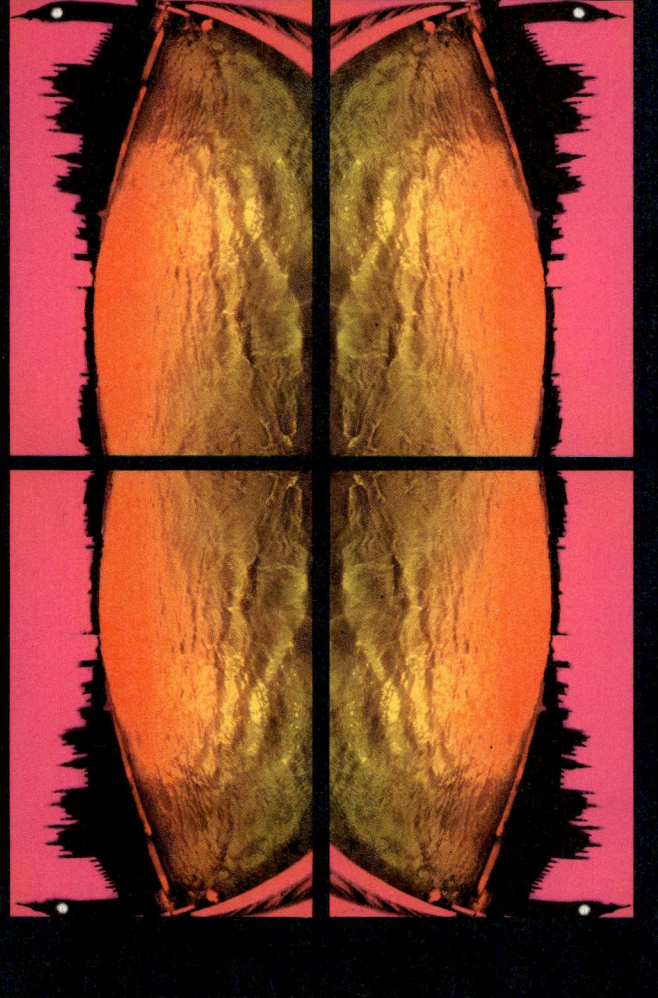

Penguin Books Ltd, Harmondsworth,
Middlesex, England
Penguin Books Inc, 7110 Ambassador Road,
Baltimore, Md 21207, USA
Penguin Books Australia Ltd,
Ringwood, Victoria, Australia

First published 1973
This selection copyright © David Jackson and Dennis Pepper, 1973

Printed in Great Britain by
Ebenezer Baylis & Son Ltd, Worcester and London
Filmset in Lumitype Baskerville by Butler & Tanner Ltd,
Frome and London

Contents

Two Tales of the Hodja

One Friday Nasreddin Hodja mounted the *mimbar* or pulpit in the mosque of Ak-Shehir to give the sermon.

'O true believers, do you know what I am going to talk to you about today?' he asked.

The congregation looked at each other in some surprise, then shook their heads.

'We have no idea,' they said.

'If you have no idea,' said the Hodja, 'what is the use of my talking to you?'

With that he descended from the *mimbar* and went home.

The following Friday he entered the mosque, mounted the *mimbar* and again asked the congregation:

'O true believers, do you know what I am going to talk to you about today?'

'Yes,' said the wily ones.

'Well, if you already know,' said the Hodja, 'what is the use of my telling you?'

And again he descended from the *mimbar* and went home.

When he again entered the mosque, he mounted the *mimbar* and asked the same question:

'O true believers, do you know what I am going to talk to you about today?'

The congregation had long since prepared their reply.

'Some of us do, and some of us do not,' they said.

'In that case,' said the Hodja, 'let those who do tell those who do not.'

And away he went.

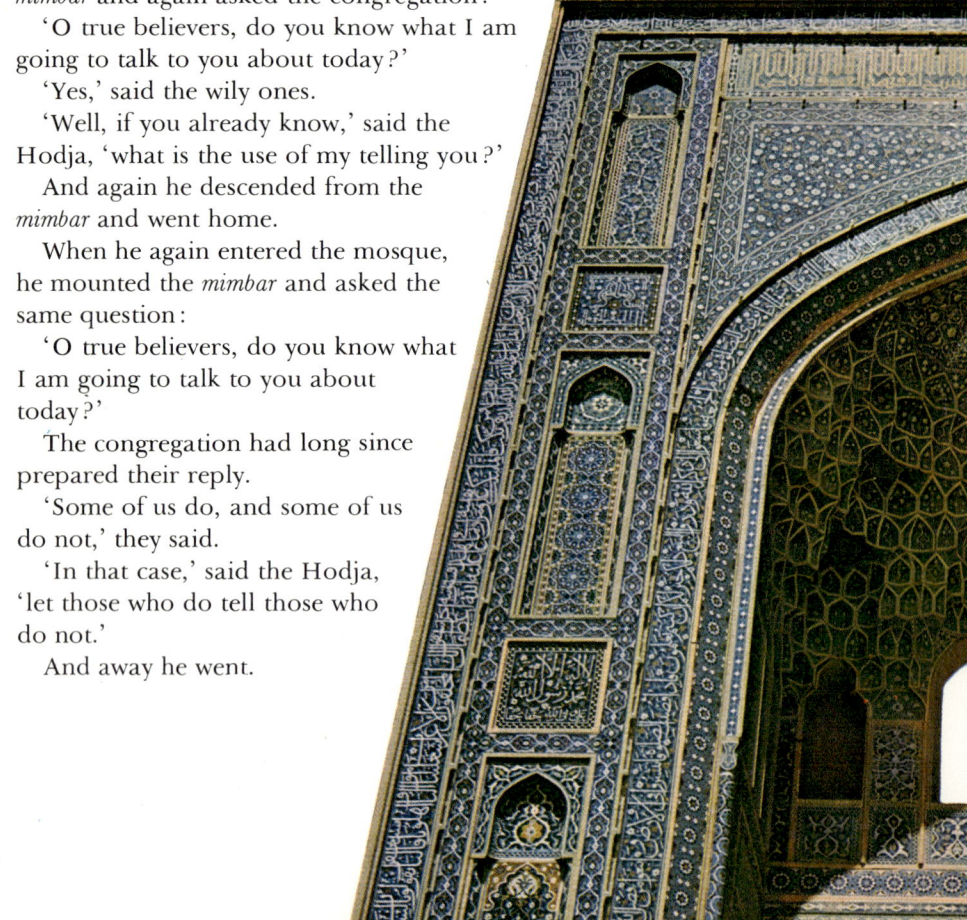

The Hodja was walking home when a man came up behind him and gave him a thump on the back of the head. When the Hodja turned round, the man began to apologize, saying that he had taken him for a friend of his. The Hodja, however, was very angry at this assault upon his dignity and dragged the man off to the court. It

Muslim judge

happened, however, that his assailant was a close friend of the *cadi* and after listening to the two parties in the dispute, the *cadi* said to his friend:

'You are in the wrong. You shall pay the Hodja a farthing damages.'

His friend said he had not that amount of money on him, and went off, saying he would fetch it. Hodja waited and waited, and still the man did not return. When an hour had passed, the Hodja got up and gave the *cadi* a mighty thump on the back of his head. 'I can wait no longer,' he said. 'When he comes, the farthing is yours.'

CHARLES DOWNING

Il mio verso sarà se mi voltate.

Axe Porridge

An old soldier was once on his way home for his leave, and he was tired and hungry. He reached a village and he rapped at the first hut.

'Let a traveller in for the night,' said he.

The door was opened by an old woman.

'Come in, soldier,' she offered.

'Have you a bite of food for a hungry man, good dame?' the soldier asked.

Now the old woman had plenty of everything, but she was stingy and pretended to be very poor.

'Ah, me, I've had nothing to eat myself today, dear heart, there is nothing in the house,' she wailed.

'Well, if you've nothing, you've nothing,' the soldier said. Then, noticing an axe without a handle under the bench: 'If there's nothing else, we could make porridge out of that axe.'

The old woman raised both hands in astonishment.

'Axe porridge? Who ever heard the like!'

'I'll show you how to make it. Just give me a pot.'

The old woman brought a pot, and the soldier washed the axe, put it in the pot, and filling the pot with water, placed it on the fire.

The soldier got out a spoon and stirred the water and then tasted it.

'It will soon be ready,' said he. 'A pity there's no salt.'

'Oh, I have salt. Here, take some.'

The soldier put some salt in the pot and then tried the water again.

'If we could just add a handful of groats to it,' said he.

The old woman brought a small bag of groats from the pantry.

'Here, add as much as you need,' said she.

The soldier went on with his cooking, stirring the meal from time to time and tasting it. And the old woman watched, and could not tear her eyes away.

'Oh, how tasty this porridge is!' the soldier said, trying a spoon-ful. 'With a bit of butter there would be nothing more delicious.'

The old woman found some butter too, and. they buttered the porridge.

'Now get a spoon, good dame, and let us eat!' the soldier said.

They began eating the porridge and praising it.

'I never thought axe porridge could taste so good!' the old woman marvelled.

And the soldier ate, and laughed up his sleeve.

TRADITIONAL RUSSIAN

Unexpected
Good Fortune

Once upon a time there was a
man who did nothing all day long
– he just waited and hoped that suddenly he would meet with unexpected
good fortune and become rich in an
instant without any effort.

And thus he lived for many a year, until
one day he heard tell that there was a certain
island inhabited by people who had only one
eye.

'At last! That will be my good fortune,' thought
the man to himself. 'I'll travel to that island, I'll
catch one of these one-eyed creatures and bring him
back and show him in the market-place for a penny
a look. In a short while I shall be a rich man.'

And the more he thought about it, the more he liked
the idea.

Finally he made up his mind. He sold the little that he had,

bought a boat and set off. After a
long journey he reached the island
of the one-eyed creatures and, indeed, hardly had he stepped ashore
when he saw that the people there
really had only one eye each.
But of course the one-eyed people
noticed that here was a man with two eyes,
and a few of them got together and said:
'At last! So this will be our good fortune!
Let's catch him and show him in the market-place
for a penny a look. We'll soon be rich men!'
No sooner said than done. They seized the two-
eyed man and carried him off to the market-place,
where they showed him for a penny a look.
And that's the sort of thing that happens to people who
sit and wait for unexpected good fortune.

TRADITIONAL

11

The Boy Who Left Home to Learn Fear

A farmer had two sons. The elder was clever and knew his way around, but the younger one was stupid and good for nothing. When people saw him they said: 'That boy will give his father trouble.' It was always the elder boy who had to help his father; but if he was sent on an errand late at night and on the way he had to cross the churchyard or some other dismal place, he would plead: 'No, father, I'd rather not go, it makes me shudder.'

When the younger brother sat in a corner and heard people telling ghost stories by the fire, he couldn't understand them when they said: 'Oh, that makes me shudder!' 'Why do they always say it makes me shudder, it makes me shudder,' he asked himself, 'I can't shudder – that must be something I have to learn.'

One day his father spoke to him: 'Listen my boy, you're getting older. It's about time you started to work. Look at your brother, he earns his keep; but what do you have to offer?' 'Father, I'd like to learn something,' he answered, 'if I had my choice I'd learn to shudder; I don't know the first thing about it.' His brother grinned and thought: 'Heavens, what a fool he is! He'll never get anywhere.' The father sighed: 'You'll learn soon enough what it is to be afraid; but you won't earn a living that way.'

A few days later the father was telling the sexton his problems: 'The boy's so stupid; he won't work and can't grasp the simplest thing. Just think, when I asked him what he wanted to do, he said he was going to learn to shudder.' 'If that's all he wants,' the sexton grinned, 'I'll teach him. Leave it to me; I'll straighten him out.'

So he took the boy on and gave him the job of bell-ringer. Some days later he woke him at midnight and told him to go to the church to ring the bell. 'I'll teach him what fear is,' he thought, as he took a short cut to the tower. As the boy was about to ring the bell, he turned and saw a white shape on the stairs. 'Who's there?' he called, but the figure was silent. 'Speak up or get out. What do you want here anyway?' Expecting the boy to take him for a ghost, the sexton didn't move. So the boy shouted again: 'What do you want here? Answer me, or I'll throw you down the stairs!' But the sexton didn't take the threat seriously and stood perfectly still. The boy gave him one more chance but when he got no answer he jumped on the startled ghost and kicked him down the stairs. Then he rang the bell and went home to bed.

The sexton's wife waited patiently for her husband. After a few hours she began to worry, so she woke the boy and asked him:

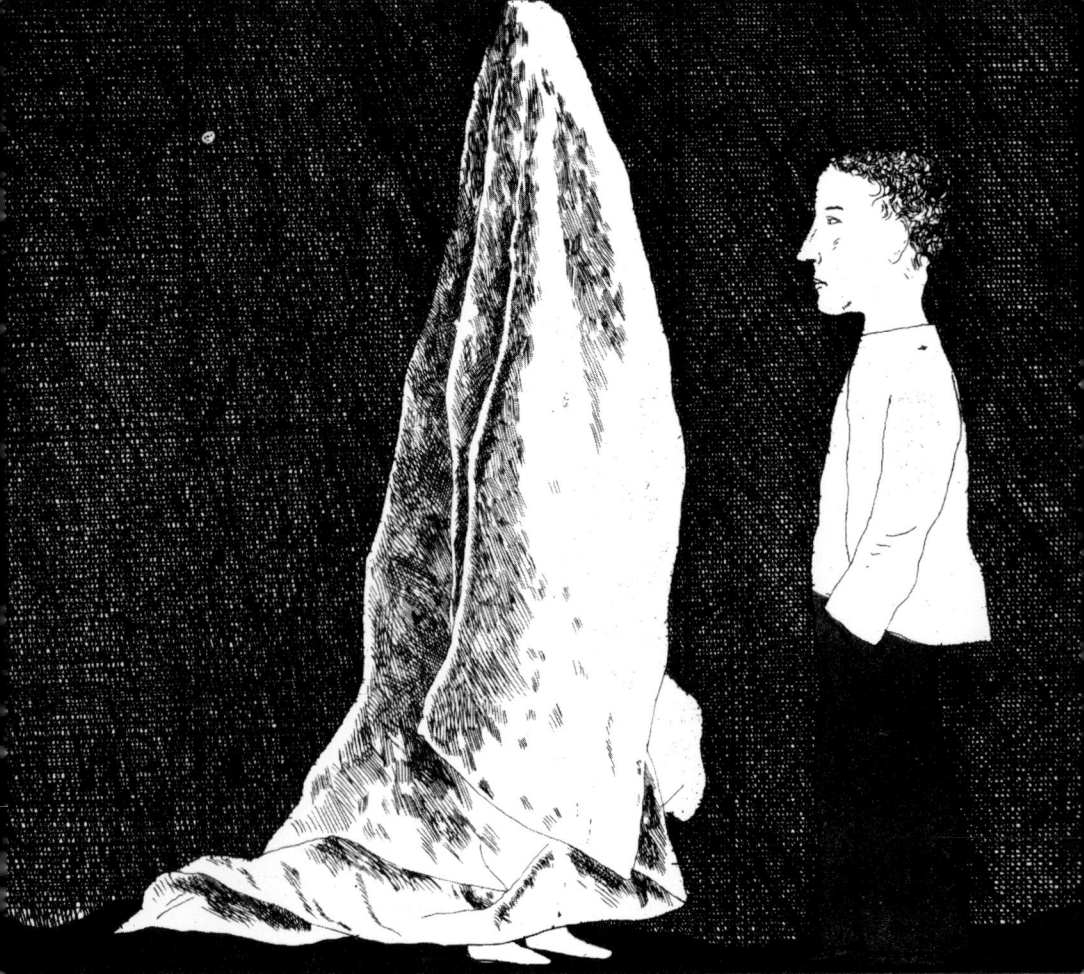

'Do you know where my husband could be? He left for the church before you.' 'I don't know,' he replied, 'but a figure in white was standing at the top of the stairs, and since he wouldn't answer me or get out of my way, I took him for a rogue and threw him to the bottom. Go and see if it's your husband, I'd be very sorry if it was. That would be bad luck.' The woman rushed to the tower and found the sexton moaning in a corner with a broken leg.

She carried him back to the house and ran screaming to the boy's father: 'Your son has kicked my husband down the stairs and broke his leg! Get him out of our house immediately!' The father was horrified and went to get the boy: 'Damn you!' he cursed. 'What mad tricks have you been up to? Are you completely off your head?' 'Listen to me, father,' he answered, 'I've done nothing wrong. It was midnight; a figure was standing there and he looked as if he were up to no good! I didn't know who it was and asked him three times either to speak up or be off.' 'Oh! my God,' his father groaned, 'you bring me nothing but trouble. Get out of my sight.' 'Well, father, I don't mind. Just let me stay until morning, then I'll go off and learn to shudder. At least that way I can earn some money.' 'Do whatever you want, I don't care. I'll give you ten pennies, then go away, the further the better. Don't tell anyone where you're from or mention my name. I'm ashamed of you.' 'Whatever you wish, father – if that's all you ask it's easy enough.'

At dawn the boy took his money and walked down to the highway, mumbling to himself: 'If only I could learn to shudder.' He passed a man who heard him talking. They walked together for a while, and when they came to a gallows, the fellow said: 'Look, this is the tree where seven men married the ropemaker's daughter; now they're learning to fly. Just stay right here and wait until nightfall, then you'll learn to shudder.' 'That's no problem,' the boy answered, 'if it's as easy as that I'll give you every penny I have. Come back tomorrow morning.'

The boy sat down by the gallows. When night fell he lit a fire, but around midnight he began to feel cold. A strong wind was blowing and the corpses bounced against one another as they swung back and forth. The boy looked up at them and thought: 'If I'm cold down here by the fire, they must really be freezing up there.' He was sorry for them so he climbed up a ladder, cut them down one by one and propped them up around the roaring fire so they could warm themselves. They sat very still, and when their clothes caught fire he shouted: 'Be careful, or I'll hang you up again.' But the dead men heard nothing and their rags burned. The boy became angry and shouted louder: 'If you don't care, why should I help you? I don't want to catch fire myself,' and one after the other he hung them up again. Then he lay down by the fire and fell asleep.

In the morning the man returned to collect his money. 'Well, boy, you must know by now what it's like to shudder.' 'What do you mean, shudder? Those fellows up there wouldn't say a word and were stupid enough to let their dirty rags get burned.' At this the man knew he wasn't going to be richer that morning, so he walked away muttering to himself: 'It beats me, I've never met anybody like him before.'

As the boy went off in the other direction he sighed: 'If only I could learn to shudder!' A shepherd overheard him and asked: 'What's your name?' 'I don't know.' 'Who is your father?' 'I'm not supposed to say.' 'And what are you grumbling about?' 'Well,' answered the boy, 'I wish I could learn to shudder. But no one can show me how it's done.' 'Nonsense,' the shepherd laughed, 'come along with me. I'll find a job for you.' So the boy joined him. In the evening they came to an inn where they decided to spend the night, and as they entered the bar the boy mumbled again: 'If only I could learn to shudder.' The innkeeper heard him and winked: 'If that's what you want, I can help you out.' But his wife overheard him; 'Shut up!' she said. 'For the job you're thinking of, quite a few young men have paid with their lives. It would be a crime if such lovely eyes as his were closed for good.' But the boy interrupted her: 'I don't care how hard it is – I left home to learn to shudder and that's what I'm here for.' And he went on pleading until they told him the story.

'Not far from here is a haunted castle where great treasures are hidden; enough, people say, to make a poor man rich for life; but they are guarded by monsters and evil spirits. The King has promised his daughter to the first man who can spend three whole nights there; and it's worth the risk as the Princess is the most beautiful girl in the world. Many have gone in, but none has come out alive.'

The next morning, the boy went to see the King and asked him if he could spend three nights in the castle. The King liked his looks, so he offered him a choice of any three objects to take with him. The boy chose a fire, a lathe, and a carpenter's bench with its knife, and the King had them taken there before nightfall.

When it was dark the boy went up to the castle and built a huge fire in one of the rooms. He sat down on the lathe and put the carpenter's bench by the fire. 'If only I could learn to shudder,' he thought, 'but surely I'm wasting my time here.' At around midnight he stirred up the fire, and while he was blowing on the coals a wild

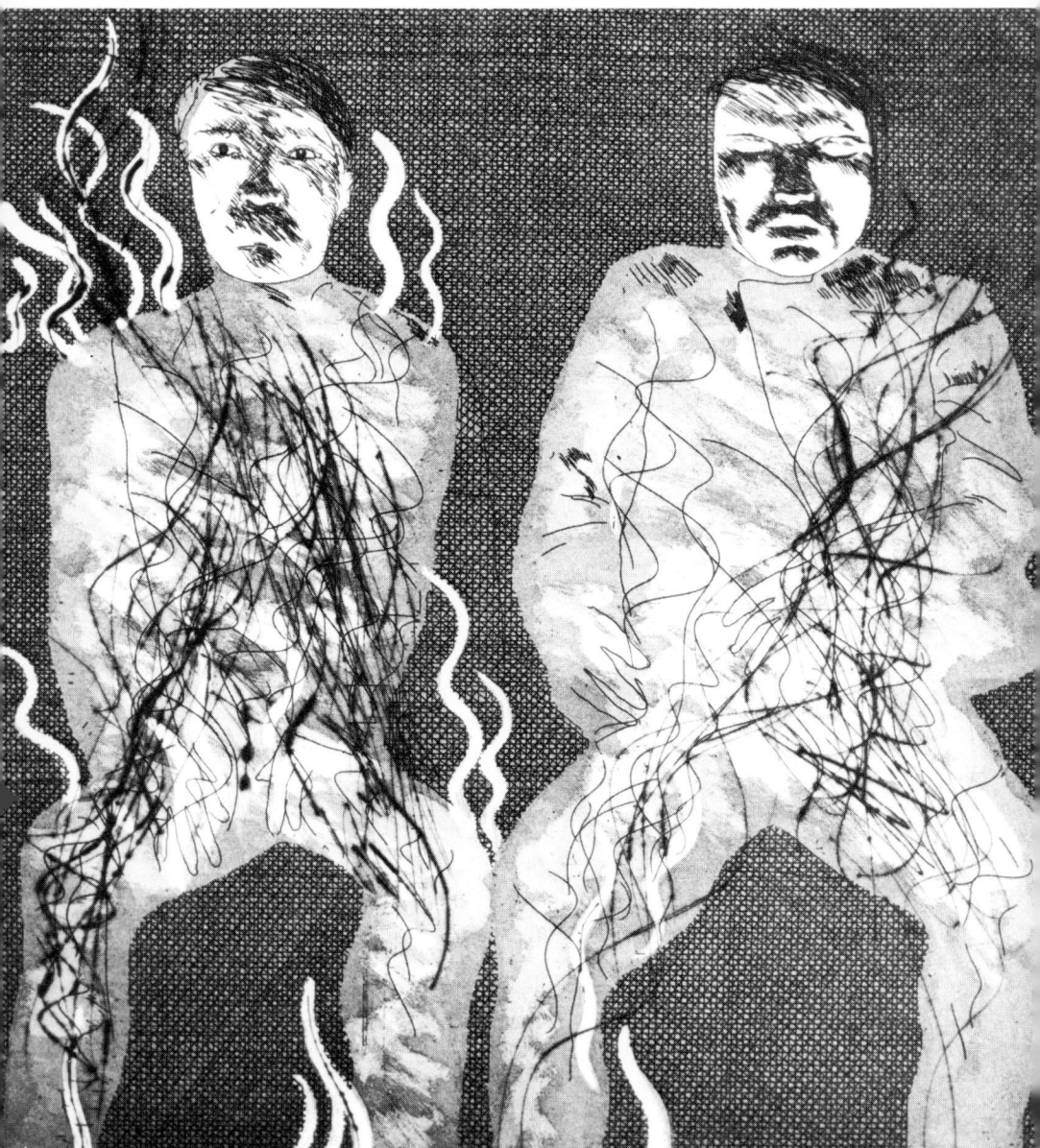

cry came up from a corner of the room. 'Aaowmeeow! We're freezing!' 'You fools, what are you complaining about? If you're cold, come and sit by me.' Two great black cats leaped out of the darkness, and sitting down on each side of the lathe glowered at him savagely with their fiery eyes. When they had warmed themselves they sneered: 'Now friend, how about a game of cards?' 'Why not!' he murmured, 'but let me see your paws first.' They stretched out their legs and he saw their long sharp claws. Then he caught them by the throat, lifted them on to the carpenter's bench and clamped their paws in the vice. 'I know your game,' he laughed, 'it's no fun playing cards with you!' So he beat them to death and threw them out into the moat.

After silencing these two, he lay down to rest. Suddenly out of every corner there rushed wild cats and dogs on red-hot chains, screeching and stamping on his fire. For a while he let them do as they pleased, but when they began to get on his nerves he cried: 'Get out of here you monsters!' and grabbing his knife he struck at them. A few escaped, but most ended up dead in the moat. The boy lay down again by the fire and fell asleep.

In the morning the King came, and when he saw the boy lying on the floor he thought the ghosts had killed him. 'It's a shame such a fine boy should be dead!' Hearing that, the boy jumped up and laughed, 'It hasn't come to that yet. One night is over, and the others will pass quickly enough.' The King was amazed and so was the innkeeper who couldn't believe his eyes. 'I didn't expect to see you again. Now do you know what it's like to shudder?' 'No, it's just a waste of my time,' the boy complained, 'if only someone could teach me!'

On the second night he walked up to the old castle, sat down beside the fire and sang the same old song: 'If only I could learn to shudder!' At ten o'clock he heard a long piercing cry. It grew louder and wilder, then stopped abruptly and all was quiet – until suddenly half a man fell down the chimney. 'Hey, are you real? Where's your other half?' The shrieking started again and moments later the other half dropped at his feet.

'Wait a minute, I'll get a good fire going for you.' When the flames were high, he turned and saw that the two halves had joined together to make a giant figure sitting on his bench. 'That's not part of the bargain,' the boy shouted, 'that's my bench.' He struggled with the giant and threw him to the ground; but as they wrestled in a corner they fell on nine thigh bones and two skulls, so the boy challenged the monster to a game of skittles. He took the skulls, put them in a lathe and turned them till they were round. 'Now we'll

have some fun,' he laughed. They played until the clock struck twelve and then the giant vanished. The boy lay down by the fire and fell asleep.

On the third night he returned to his bench. Towards midnight six giants walked in carrying a coffin. 'This must be my little cousin', he thought, 'who died just a few days ago.' When they put the coffin down, he lifted the lid. There was a dead man inside, his face as cold as ice; so he lifted the body out and, sitting down by the fire, laid him in his lap. He rubbed the corpse to get the blood circulating, but it didn't help, so he put the body into his bed, got a blanket and lay down beside it; after a while the corpse warmed up and began to move. The boy was delighted and whispered to him: 'See what I've done for you, little cousin!' But the dead man put his hands round the boy's neck and tried to strangle him. 'Is that how you thank me?' he shouted, 'away with you,' and grabbing the

body he threw it into the box and slammed down the lid. The six giants lifted the coffin on to their shoulders and carried it away.

Soon after the walls began to shake and split apart, and in the smoke there appeared a magnificent old giant with a long white beard. 'Boy,' he thundered, 'you'll soon know what it's like to shudder. You're going to die!' 'We'll see who's going to die,' the boy answered. 'Yes, we'll see,' the giant sneered, 'if you're the stronger I'll let you go.' He led the way through a dark tunnel to a blacksmith's forge, where he took an axe and with two blows drove an anvil deep into the ground. 'That's nothing,' grinned the boy, walking over with him to another anvil. He split it with a single blow, catching the monster's beard in the crack. 'Now I have you,' he laughed, 'it's your turn to die.' With an iron bar he thrashed the giant until he begged and pleaded with him to stop, promising him a great reward; so the boy set him free. They returned to the castle, where the giant unlocked a cellar door and showed him three chests of gold: 'One is for the poor, the second for the King, and the third is yours.' Just then the clock struck twelve and the giant vanished leaving the boy in total darkness. Next morning the King came and asked what had happened. 'My dead cousin came to see me and an old bearded fellow showed me three treasure chests in the cellar; but no one taught me to shudder.' The King was overjoyed: 'You have saved the castle,' he cried, 'now you may marry my daughter.'

The young Prince loved his wife but he still complained: 'If only I could learn to shudder!' At last the Princess's maid had an idea: she went out to a stream and caught a bucketful of fish. When the Prince was asleep she pulled his blankets back and poured the cold water with the little fish into his bed so that they squirmed and flopped all around him. The Prince sprang up: 'My God,' he cried, 'why do I shudder so?'

THE BROTHERS GRIMM

Translated from the German by Heiner Bastian

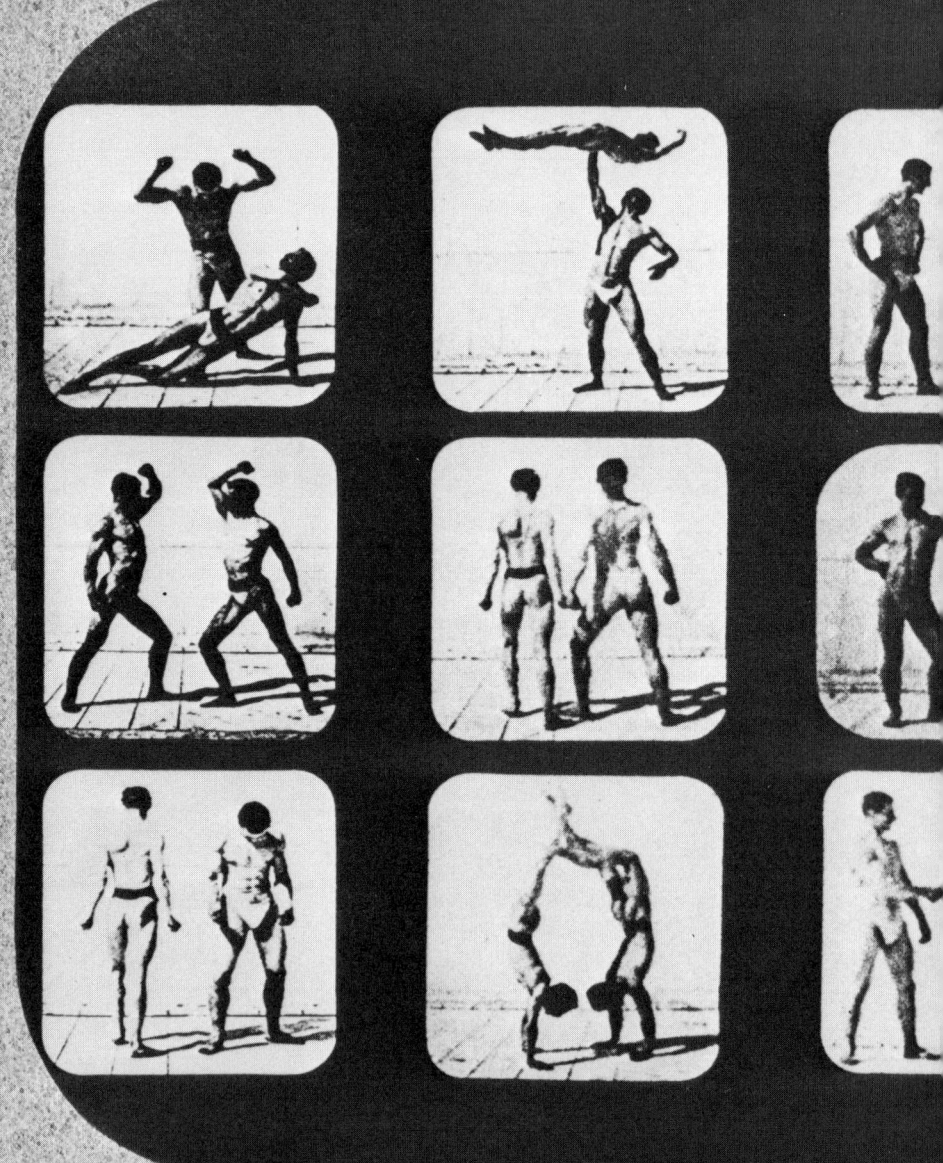

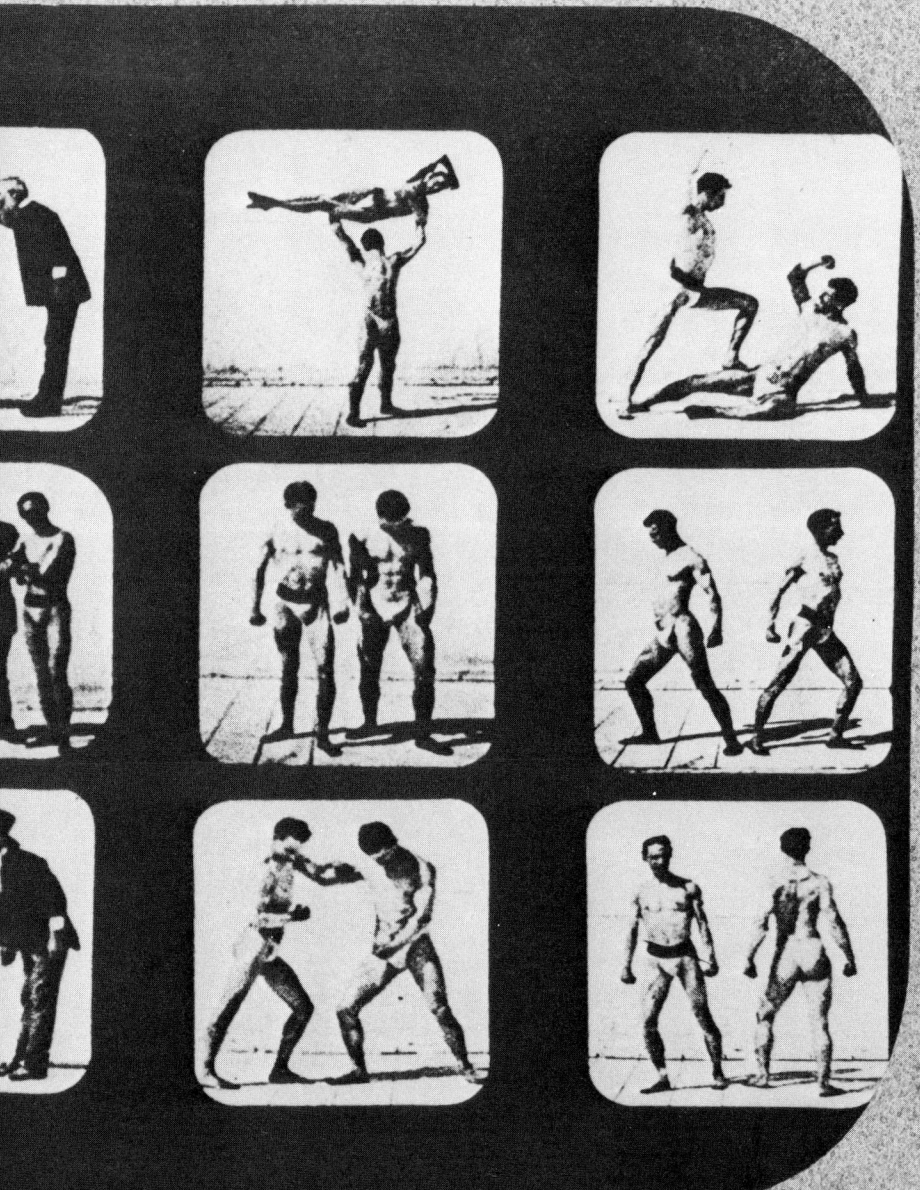

The Glass in the Field

A short time ago some builders, working on a studio in Connecticut, left a huge square of plate glass standing upright in a field one day. A goldfinch flying swiftly across the field struck the glass and was knocked cold. When he came to he hastened to his club, where an attendant bandaged his head and gave him a stiff drink. 'What the hell happened?' asked a sea gull. 'I was flying across a meadow when all of a sudden the air crystallized on me,' said the goldfinch. The sea gull, and a hawk, and an eagle all laughed heartily. A swallow listened gravely. 'For fifteen years, fledgling and bird, I've flown this country,' said the eagle, 'and I assure you there is no such thing as air crystallizing. Water, yes; air, no.' 'You were probably struck by a hailstone,' the hawk told the goldfinch. 'Or he may have had a stroke,' said the sea gull. 'What do you think, swallow?' 'Why, I – I think maybe the air crystallized on him,' said the swallow. The large birds laughed so loudly that the goldfinch became annoyed and bet them each a dozen worms that they couldn't follow the course he had flown across the field without encountering the hardened atmosphere. They all took his bet; the swallow went along to watch. The sea gull, the eagle, and the hawk decided to fly together over the route the goldfinch indicated. 'You come, too,' they said to the swallow. 'I – I – well, no,' said the swallow. 'I don't think I will.' So the three large birds took off together and they hit the glass together and they were all knocked cold.

Moral: He who hesitates is sometimes saved.

JAMES THURBER

Pueblo, Colorado, 4 July 1905: Here in an early action shot is the afternoon plunge of Eunice Winkless, a daring amateur who, said the local paper, clung 'to the mane as the horse dived headlong ... to the pool of water below' and 'emerged dripping' (how else?) to claim her prize of $100.

A Table is a Table

I want to tell the story of an old man, of a man who has given up talking, who has a tired face, too tired for smiling and too tired for frowning. He lives in a small town, at the end of the street or near the crossroads. It's hardly worth while to describe him, so little distinguishes him from others. He wears a grey hat, grey trousers, a grey jacket and in winter his long grey overcoat, and he has a thin neck whose skin is dry and wrinkled, his white shirt collars are far too wide for him.

His room is up on the top floor of the house, maybe he was once married and had children, maybe he used to live in a different town. Certainly he was once a child, but that was at a time when children were dressed like adults. You can see them like that in Granny's photograph album. In his room there are two chairs, a table, a carpet, a bed and a wardrobe. An alarm clock stands on a little table, next to it lie old newspapers, and the photograph album, a mirror and a picture hang on the wall.

In the morning the old man took a walk, and another in the afternoon, exchanging a few words with his neighbour, and in the evening he sat at his table.

This never changed, even on Sundays it was the same. And when the man sat at the table he heard the alarm clock tick, always he heard the alarm clock tick.

Then suddenly came a special day, a day with sunshine, not too hot, not too cold, with birds twittering, with friendly people, with children who were playing – and the special thing about it was that for once it all pleased the man.

He smiled.

'Now everything is going to change,' he thought. He undid his top shirt button, seized his hat, accelerated his pace, went so far as to make his knees flex as he walked, and was glad. He came back to his street, nodded to the children, walked up to his house, climbed the stairs, took his keys out of his pocket and unlocked his room.

But in his room everything was the same, a table, two chairs, a bed. And as he sat down he heard that ticking again, and all the gladness went out of him, for nothing had changed.

And a great rage took possession of the man.

In the mirror he saw his face flush, as he narrowed his eyes; then he clenched his hands, raised them and brought them down on the table-top, only one blow at first, then another, and then he started to drum on the table, while he cried out again and again:

'It's got to change, it's got to change.'

And he no longer heard the alarm clock. Then his hands began to hurt, his voice failed, then he heard the alarm clock again and nothing changed.

'Always the same table,' said the man, 'the same chairs, the bed, the picture. And the table I call table, the picture I call picture, the bed is called bed, and the chair is called chair. Why, come to think of it? The French call a bed "lee", a table "tahbl", call a picture "tahblow" and a chair "shaze", and they understand each other. And the Chinese understand each other too.'

'Why isn't the bed called picture?' thought the man, and smiled, then he laughed, laughed till the neighbours banged on the wall and shouted 'Quiet!'

'Now things are going to change,' he cried out, and from now on he called the bed 'picture'.

'I'm tired, I want to go to picture,' he said, and often in the morning he would lie in picture for a long time, wondering what he would now call the chair, and he called the chair 'alarm clock'.

So he got up, dressed, sat down on his alarm clock and rested his arms on the table. But the table was no longer called table, it was now called carpet. So in the morning the man left his picture, got dressed, sat down at the carpet on the alarm clock and wondered what to call what.

He called the bed picture.

He called the table carpet.

He called the chair alarm clock.

He called the newspaper bed.

He called the mirror chair.

He called the alarm clock photograph album.

He call the wardrobe newspaper.

He called the carpet wardrobe.

He called the picture table.

And he called the photograph album mirror.

So:

In the morning the old man would lie in picture for a long time, at nine the photograph album rang, the man got up and stood on the wardrobe, so that his feet wouldn't feel cold, then he took his clothes out of the newspaper, dressed, looked into the chair on the wall, then sat down on the alarm clock at the carpet and turned the pages of the mirror until he found his mother's table.

The man thought this was fun, and he practised all day long and impressed the words on his memory. Now he gave everything new names: Now he was no longer a man, but a foot, and the foot was a morning and the morning a man.

Now you can continue the story for yourselves. And then, like the man, you can change the other words round:

to ring is to stand,

to feel cold is to look,

to lie is to ring,

to get up is to feel cold,

to stand is to turn over the pages.

So we get this:

In the man the old foot would ring in picture for a long time, at nine the photograph album stood, the foot felt cold and turned over the pages on the wardrobe, so that his mornings would not look.

The old man bought himself blue exercise books and filled them with the new words, and it kept him very busy, and now he was rarely seen in the street.

Then he learned the new names for all kinds of things and forgot the right ones more and more. He now had a new language that belonged to him alone.

Now and again he began to dream in the new language, and then he translated the songs of his school days into his own language and sang them softly to himself.

But soon even translating became difficult for him, he had almost forgotten his old language, and he had to look for the right words in his blue exercise books. And he was frightened of talking to people. He had to search his mind for a long time for the names that people call things.

His picture people call bed.

His carpet people call table.

His alarm clock people call chair.

His bed people call newspaper.

His chair people call mirror.

His photograph album people call alarm clock.

His newspaper people call wardrobe.

His wardrobe people call carpet.

His table people call picture.

His mirror people call photograph album. And it went so far that the man couldn't help laughing when he heard people talk.

He couldn't help laughing when he heard someone say:

'Will you be going to the football match tomorrow?' Or when someone said: 'It's been raining for two months.' Or when someone said: 'I've got an uncle in America.'

He couldn't help laughing because he didn't understand a word of it.

But this is not a cheerful story. It began sadly and ends sadly too.

The old man in the grey coat couldn't understand people any more; that wasn't so bad.

What was much worse, they couldn't understand him any more.

And that's why he gave up talking.

He kept quiet,
spoke only to himself,
no longer so much as nodded to people when
he passed them.

PETER BICHSEL

Translated from the German by Michael Hamburger

The Man Who Didn't Want
to Know Any More

'I don't want to know any more,' said the man who didn't want to know any more.

The man who didn't want to know any more said: 'I don't want to know any more.'

That's easily said.

That's easily said.

And already the telephone rings.

And instead of ripping the wires out of the wall, as he should have done, because he didn't want to know any more, he lifted the receiver and said his name.

'Good morning,' said the other.

And the man also said: 'Good morning.'

'Fine weather we're having,' said the other.

And the man didn't say: 'I don't want to know about that,' he even said: 'Yes indeed, it's lovely weather.'

And the other said something else.

And the man said something else.

And then the man put back the receiver and was very angry because now he knew that the weather was fine.

And now he did rip the wires out of the wall and shouted: 'I don't want to know that either, I want to forget it.'

That's easily said.

That's easily said.

For the sun shone through the window, and when the sun shines through the window one knows that the weather is fine.

The man closed the shutters, but now the sun shone through the chinks.

The man fetched paper and stuck it on the window panes and sat in the dark.

And he sat like that for a long time, and his wife came and saw the covered windows and was startled. She asked: 'What's that for?'

'That's for keeping the sun out,' said the man.

'Then you'll have no light,' said his wife.

'That's a drawback,' said the man, 'but it's better like that, for if I have no sunlight I'm in the dark, true enough, but at least I don't know that the weather is fine.'

'What have you got against fine weather?' said his wife. 'Fine weather cheers people up.'

'I have nothing against fine weather,' said the man. 'I have nothing against any sort of weather at all, I just don't want to know what it's like.'

'In that case at least turn on the light,' said his wife, and she made to turn it on, but the man ripped the lamp out of the ceiling and said: 'I don't want to know that either, I don't want to know any more that you can turn on the light.'

At that his wife burst into tears.

And the man said: 'You see, I don't want to know anything any more.'

And because his wife could not understand that, she stopped crying and left her husband in the dark.

And there he stayed for a very long time.

And people who called on them asked the wife where her husband was, and the wife explained: 'It's like this you see, he sits in the dark, you see, and doesn't want to know anything any more, you see.'

'What doesn't he want to know any more?' the people asked, and the wife replied:

'Anything. He doesn't want to know anything any more. He doesn't want to know what he sees – what the weather is like, for instance.

'He doesn't want to know what he hears – what people say, for instance.

'And he doesn't want to know what he knows – how you turn on the light, for instance.

'That's how it is, you see,' said the wife.

'Ah, so that's how it is,' said the people, and they didn't call again.

And the man sat in the dark.

And his wife brought him his meals.

And she asked him: 'What don't you know any more?'

And he said: 'I still know everything,' and he was very sad because he still knew everything.

Then his wife tried to console him and said: 'But you don't know what the weather is like, do you?'

'I don't know what it's like,' said the man, 'but I still know what it can be like. I still remember rainy days, and I still remember sunny days.'

'You'll forget it,' said the wife.

And the man said: 'That's easily said.

That's easily said.'

And he remained in the dark, and his wife brought him his meals each day, and the man looked at the plate and said: 'I know that those are potatoes, I know that that is meat, and I know cauliflower; and it's all no use, I shall always know everything. And I know every word I speak.'

And when next his wife asked him: 'What do you still know?' he said: 'I know much more than before, I don't only know what fine weather and bad weather are like, I now know too what no weather at all is like. And I know that when it's quite dark it still isn't dark enough.'

'But there *are* things you don't know,' said his wife and wanted to go, and when he held her back she said: 'I mean, you don't know what "*fine weather*" is called in Chinese,' and she went and shut the door behind her.

Then the man who didn't want to know any more began to think hard. He really didn't know Chinese, and it was no good his saying: 'I don't want to know that either any more,' because he never had known it.

'First I have to know what I don't want to know,' the man exclaimed and tore open the window and opened the shutters, and in front of the window it was raining, and he gazed into the rain.

Then he went into town to buy books about Chinese, and he came back and sat for weeks over those books and painted Chinese ideograms on paper.

symbols

And when people called and asked the wife about her husband, she said: 'It's like this, you see, he's now learning Chinese, you see, that's how it is, you see.'

And those people didn't call again.

But it takes months and years to learn Chinese, and when at last he had learnt it, he said:

'But I still don't know enough. I have to know everything. Only then I shall be able to say that I don't want to know all that any more.

'I have to know what wine tastes like, what bad wine tastes like and what good wine tastes like.

'And when I eat potatoes I must know how they are planted.

'I must know what the moon looks like, for when I see it I'm still far from knowing what it looks like, and I must know how to get to it.

'And I must know the names of animals and what they look like and what they do and where they live.'

And he bought a book about rabbits and a book about hens and a book about animals in the wild and another about insects.

And then he bought a book about the white rhinoceros.

He went to the zoo and found it there, and it was in a large en-closure and did not move.

And the man saw exactly how the white rhinoceros tried to think and tried to know something, and he saw what an effort it cost the rhinoceros.

And every time something occurred to the white rhinoceros it ran off with joy, did two or three circuits around the enclosure and, doing so, forgot what had occurred to it, and then remained stand-ing for a long time – an hour, two hours – and ran off again when the same thing occurred to it again.

And because it always ran off a little bit too soon, really nothing occurred to it at all.

'A white rhinoceros is what I should like to be,' said the man, 'but I suppose it's too late for that.'

Then he went home and thought about his rhinoceros.

And he now spoke of nothing else.

'My white rhinoceros,' he said, 'thinks too slowly and runs off too soon, and that's how it should be,' and that made him forget all the things he wanted to know in order not to know them any more.

And he began to live again as he had lived before.

Except that he now knew Chinese.

PETER BICHSEL
Translated from the German by Michael Hamburger

Girlie Christian's Missing Leg

WHICKER   You see, last time I saw you, you came galloping out to meet me on a horse, I remember.

GIRLIE   Yes, that was up Middlegate.

WHICKER   That was ten years ago.

GIRLIE   Yes.

WHICKER   Since then you've had this unhappy accident.

GIRLIE   Oh yes.

WHICKER   How did that happen?

GIRLIE   Well, I pretty well lived on horseback, and I was going off to get ripe peaches this time, and a big chestnut horse came up. It was his turn to go out for a gallop, so I saddled up and was going down to get peaches. He's been down there a million times before, but this time he didn't want to go down. So I told him he'd damn well gotta get down. 'Go on,' I said. 'Get down there.' And wuff, he turned round and bucked, and I shot up in the air as if I should have been an angel with wings. I thought I would never stop flying, and I've never been able to stand up ever since, without a great struggle. But I've always had somebody, one on each arm, to drag me up. The doctors told me to get out and grow up or else I'll never be able to move again – but I was quite determined. I think I've got some of Christian's spirit in me. By golly I do struggle for that to get round, and I'm very thankful to be alive and can get up at all.

WHICKER   You were flying through the air when you'd been thrown from the horse. What happened to you then?

GIRLIE   Well I hit the ground harder than I wanted to, and in the struggle I was lying there for a long time. So I wondered what was happening and I turned round and looked to see where the horse was, and there he was, with his hind legs way up in the air, bucking and fighting and jumping in the air. I've never seen any cowboys go through such a performance on the pictures.

WHICKER   And you were underneath, were you?

GIRLIE   Well, worse was to come.

WHICKER   How?

GIRLIE   When I looked up, he was straight up in the air, and he couldn't go back. He came straight down, saddle and all over me. I was nearly killed. He came down over me and he was laying down across my body, just my forehead and my eyes, I could see what was going on. He was kicking four legs sideways like that, and we were rolling down the hill at the same time, and I blocked him from rolling somewhat. And then he was kicking and he got a footing, and then, he stood up like this on his front legs. His body was crushing my chest and my stomach – boy, I must have been strong. The Doctor said I was made of iron. So when he got a footing on his front legs, he propped up and got off me and ran away, and I couldn't move then for a long time. I don't know how long it was, but I laid there thinking, 'Oh, if I don't get out of this I'm going to die, and I'll be jiggered if I'm going to die here and sleep down here with these ants. I'm going to get up and go home. I tried to get up but I couldn't get up. I tried to put my hands to go forward and then I turned slowly to try and crawl. Then, I thought, well there's something wrong – everything's dead and free-like. So I turned round to try and find what's wrong. There was my leg over there on the ground, and the bone stuck down in the ground.

WHICKER   Your leg?

GIRLIE   This right leg was over there on the ground. And all I thought of – well, I'll jolly well have to take that leg, get it up the hill somehow and take it to the hospital. Crawl up and wait on the side of the road till someone comes and picks me up and takes me to hospital. I want it to be sewn on because I want to go to the old ballroom and see the old dances. So I struggled round and I gradually reached for my leg. I took it up in my right hand and with this leg swimming in the blood I crawled up the hill till I was outside on the bank. I was lying there for a while and that man up there at the party with that beard came. And I tell you this little man who took me to hospital he came round and he found me there. I said, 'My spirit was calling you, I wanted you,' I said, 'I was longing for you to come around that corner and you did come.' He said, 'Well, your spirit must have been calling me.' I said it was, you're the very one, because you've got this old truck, because I couldn't get in a car, I was too hurt. And when he came up there he was passing, and I called 'Hey.' He said 'Hello.' So when he didn't stop I sat down and shouted as loud as I could, 'Hey, get back here.' He turned round and was quite annoyed, 'What's the matter with you?' 'Get out of that car and come down here and see.' 'What, where?' he said. 'Well,' I said, 'look down there.' I had taken the foot and put it down near there. He looked down and saw this thing separated. Well, his face went as white as a man's clean white shirt. 'There,'

I said, 'that's what's the matter.' And I said, 'you slide me on the truck.' Well, we had several tries and I screamed and he had to put me down. 'Hang on a minute,' I said, 'I'll put my hand up there now and slide me up. Slide me up, get me and slide me up.' So I got on. He took me round. I was nearly going out on the way and I didn't want to go out so I shook myself up by looking up to see how far we had got to, to keep myself from thinking. So when we got up there I heard him call, 'Hey mate, someone's hurt; come here.' And all of a sudden a whole pile of them came and one with a bit of cloth. I asked him to put one of them sack-bags round my foot. 'No,' he said, 'the dust will get in it.' I said, 'There's plenty of dirt and dust in it already, so he took me round.' Oh, they were wonderful and I found Doctor Clark there. He was only a short man. I said, 'Who is this doll looking at us?' One of them said, 'Girlie, be careful that's Doctor Clark from England.' 'No he isn't. He a schoolboy. You don't kid me.' And he kept looking at me. I said, 'Yea, you summing me up. I'll sum you up if you don't look out.' And one of them came over to me and shook me and said, 'Girlie, that's the Doctor.' I looked at him, I said, 'Go ahead, hurry up, put me out.' I said, 'I've got every confidence in you.' He was beautiful, beautiful, I couldn't have had a better doctor in all the world than what he was. I said, 'Doc, before I go under, sew my leg on again so's I can go to the ballroom.' So I said, 'I'm old and ugly but still I like the ballrooms. They suit me good there. They're beautiful.' So he said, 'Right, I'll sew your leg on.' If it wasn't for the promise he made to sew my leg on I would have been well and got over my accident quicker. But my word, a different one passed me and said, 'He should have taken it off right away.' 'Oh no.' I said, 'It was my fault and he was beautiful. He did nothing wrong and he was beautiful, all the nurses were beautiful. I couldn't get better anywhere.'

WHICKER Now, how have you managed to get around on only one leg since then?

GIRLIE I get around just as best way I can. I sometimes hop, I sometimes fall, but it takes me an hour to get up, to struggle up.

WHICKER You haven't done much riding since then, have you?

GIRLIE I haven't been able to get off the ground leave alone get up on a horse any more. I saw one up there this morning, it nearly sent me crying. I wanted to go out again, but it's my back that's hurt. I was bruised and such all inside. I've never stopped aching since.

EXTRACT FROM AN INTERVIEW WITH ALAN WHICKER

Simon Rodia,
Architect and
Builder of the
Watts Towers

'I no have anybody help
me out.
I was a poor man.
Had to do a little at a time.
Nobody helped me.
I think if I hire a man.
he don't know what to do.
A million times
I don't know what
to do myself.
I never had a single helper.
Some of the people say
what was he doing . . .
some of the people
think I was crazy
and some people said
I was going to do something.
I wanted to do something
in the United States
because I was raised here
you understand?
I wanted to do something
for the United States
because there are nice people
in this country.'

SIMON RODIA

The Towers and their Maker

The steep open structures loom from a flat and colourless neighbourhood in the southwest section of Los Angeles. Oil derricks? Gothic cathedral? They are a construction of steel rods, mesh and mortar, in a maze of forms which soar to a hundred-foot height. The weblike members are covered with a glittering encrustation of broken tiles, dishes, bottles and seashells. Woven together by overhead arches around the spires are fountains, pavilions and labyrinths. This walled magic garden is covered, too, with multicoloured mosaic, or with imprints of tools, hands, corncobs and baskets, interwoven here and there with the initials of their builder, a poor tile-setter who had in his mind for thirty years to do something big, to have his fingerprint on this obscure corner of the world.

One man – Simon Rodia – created the Towers without aid in

47

thirty-three intensely purposeful years. He worked with no drawing-board designs, machine equipment, or scaffolding. The structures were literally 'built in the air', using only the simple tools of a tile-setter, together with window-washer's belt and bucket. In gathering materials, Simon collected more than 70,000 seashells, dismantled pipe structures and steel bed-frames, and salvaged countless tiles and bottles. As the work progressed, his ideas changed, and the Towers were revised and elaborated. 'How could I have help?' said Simon. 'I couldn't tell anyone what to do . . . cause most of the time I didn't know what to do myself.' In 1954, work done, he deeded his lot and his Towers to a neighbour and went away.

Simon was more than forty years old when he began the Towers; why did he set himself such a staggering task? His life story helps to explain him. Born in 1879 in Rome, he came to the United States before he was twelve. Not much is known of his early years. He worked in logging and mining camps, held jobs as a night watch-man and construction worker, and was employed in Los Angeles as a tile-setter and telephone repairman. He bought a house and lot in Watts where his Spanish-speaking neighbours knew him as Sam Rodilla. In his cherished *Encyclopaedia Britannica* he read of heroes – men like Marco Polo, Columbus and Galileo. Once he remarked, 'You have to be good good or bad bad to be remembered.' And again, referring to his Towers, 'I had in mind to do something big, and I did.'

Having finished the Towers, why did he leave? Some feel that like every great artist, Simon's needs were satisfied in the doing. Once the Towers were done, they say, he no longer needed them. Others feel he left because of some strong disappointment. Discovered living in Martinez, California, in 1959, Simon was reluctant even to talk about the Towers. 'If your mother dies and you have loved her very much,' he said, 'maybe you don't speak of her.'

ANONYMOUS

The Woodwose

The oldest man, a leader of men,
answered; he unlocked the wordhoard.

Cealla looked up from the new furrows he was planting with winter corn, and frowned as the children came running from the golden wood, calling to each other, and to him, in high screaming voices.

'Where's the firewood?' he demanded, seeing their empty hands.

'We couldn't get it,' said Wulfrun, lifting her thin face to him, and returning his gaze, unashamed.

Cealla's temper snapped. 'By all the gods, you brats deserve a flogging!' he cried. 'I and your mother, Wulfrun, and your mother and father, Beorn, and yours, and yours, bend over plough and harrow in the fields day after day, slaving to bring in food for your greedy gullets, and you, feckless and useless idlers, will not even bring kindling for the fires!'

The little group of children fell silent, moved closer to one another.

'You will remember one day, with bitterness in your hearts, the times when you had nothing to do but go gathering in the woods!' he lamented, for his back and arms were aching.

'There was a bear there,' said Totta, the youngest boy, 'and so we were frightened and ran home.'

'Freya strikes dumb those who lie,' cried Cealla, his anger cold now. 'Go back and bring wood, or the supper pots will be cold.'

But the children stood still. They shrank a little from his anger, but they did not move back towards the wood. They glanced over their shoulders at the line of russet branches, and the dark tunnels between the tree-trunks, where the wood began, and they stayed still.

'There *was* a bear,' said Beorn, the oldest of them. 'We found its smelly lair, and then it came and chased us, and it was black, and shaggy, and it roared at us.'

'Get you gone!' cried Cealla. 'Do I not know that there have been no bears in these woods in our time or our fathers' time? I shall drive you to work with my belt across your backs if you take not your lying tongues out of my reach!'

The children fled, each one running for his own parents' door. Only Wulfrun, who had nowhere to run to, since Cealla was her father, was left.

'But there *was* a bear. I saw it,' she said.

Cealla put down the basket of seed corn, and looked at his

daughter. He and his wife bewailed the girl's failings every day, but they had never had cause to call her a liar before. He sent her home to his wife, and went to find Offa his neighbour.

The story went round the village quickly, for it was only a small place. The men left the sowing and gathered to talk at the end of the village, where there was a roughly-hewn wooden boar's head set up on a pole to bring luck to their councils.

'There are two hours left until dark,' said Readda, who was the richest man. 'We had best go now, and see.'

They took nets and spears with them, and Readda, who had an iron sword, went to fetch it, and brought also his son, Totta, to tell them where to look.

Cealla had two fierce hunting dogs which he had caught and tamed himself. They were fearless against wild boar, and might even face a bear, if bear there really was. He called them to heel, and went with the other men.

'He was up by the height of the wood,' said Totta. 'We were playing by the Giants' Wall, and then we went through the gate in it, where we have never been before, and then he was there.'

'What is the Giants' Wall?' asked Cealla.

'It is a house of stone, all broken now, which stands in the woods,' said Readda. 'A cunningly-made thing. I have not been there since I was a boy.'

Cealla kept silent. He had not been able to run the woods when he himself was young. He had lived in the village all his life, and not known there was anything wonderful in the woods.

But the place made him afraid when he saw it. There was a high wall, of smooth stones, suddenly standing up among the trees. The top was ragged, and fallen stones lay all around with grass and sorrel growing over them. Drifts of old-man's-beard and dark ivy clambered over the wall. The gateway in it had a great stone lintel, supported by a pile of white stones made round, and straight like a tree trunk. Cealla shuddered to think of the might of the builders, or spells   else of their magic runes, for surely it was beyond human skill to shape the hard stone so.

But Readda walked straight through, under the tall lintel, and called the others after him. Beyond, there was a courtyard with ruined walls round it. Grass and tall thistle grew in between, and broken stone lay everywhere. In the centre was an upright wand of stripped hazel, with a little cross-piece tied to it, making the shape of a sword stuck point downwards in the ground. In one corner was a blackened ring upon the grass, where a fire had lately been lit.

'Well,' said Readda, looking round, 'now we know what kind of bear we are looking for.' He made the sign of Thor's hammer on his forehead, and then struck down the cross of twigs. 'Some go round that way, some this,' he said.

Splitting up, the men cautiously worked their way round the ruin.

Cealla and his party were nearly halfway round when cries went up from the other side. They ran to join their fellows. The others were struggling with something caught in one of their nets. The net covered a dark mass, which fought and heaved and took three men to hold down. Cealla's dogs growled, and their hackles rose, but he called them off for fear they should bite one of his friends in the confusion. It was getting dark and difficult to see.

At last some heavy blows with a branch of wood subdued the captured beast, and they slung it, still netted, on a pole to carry home.

'What is it?' whispered Cealla to the next man.

'No bear, that's certain,' he replied. 'A woodwose, and a fierce one.'

It was pitch dark when they got their catch back to the village. To keep it safe for the night they simply drove a stake through the net in which it was tied, deep into the ground. In the red flicker of their torches they could see it struggle in the net to free itself, and they could see that it was caught fast.

'It is a woodwose,' they told their wives.

'Give it water, and come away,' said Readda.

The fire in Readda's hut had burnt so low that there was nothing in the smooth black darkness except a little glowing patch of scarlet cinders.

'Mother, Mother,' whispered Totta in the dark, 'what's a wood-wose?'

demon 'A forest troll,' said his mother. 'One of those who had the land before us. Before we came.'

Creeping out of their huts in the first light of day the children saw that the bear was really a man. He had black hair, very dark, growing thickly on his arms and on his chest. But they had thought he was a bear because of the great shaggy bearskin cloak he wore around his shoulders. Now he sat squatting, and glared at them through the web of rope which held him.

'Poor thing, poor thing,' said Wulfrun softly. 'I wish we had not told about him.' But when it seemed he heard her, and turned his head to look at her, she became frightened and ran away.

'We must take him to Arnulf,' said Readda.

'Arnulf is old now,' grumbled Offa. 'His words wander. He will talk and talk.'

'He is still our lord, and lord of all this valley,' insisted Readda. 'We must go to him.'

A little procession of them formed in the village, not early in the day, for come what might the corn had to be planted, but after mid-day, when a morning's work had already been done. In the meantime the woodwose had had nothing to eat except a handful of crusts left over from Wulfrun's breakfast. They did not risk undoing the net, but carried him on a rod over their shoulders, laboriously, for Arnulf's hall was in a village higher up the valley, and the captive was not light.

lords

All the men of Arnulf's village came out to look, the women with them, and the children to their mothers' skirts. Arnulf's own thanes stood around, and Arnulf came to his door, and sat upon a chair carried out for him, and the man in the net was set down on the ground before him. Arnulf was very old now. Each time they saw him again it seemed to them he had grown older since the last time. His hair was white, and his beard hung down from his chin past his sword belt, which was not as far as it had once been, for he was bent as though carrying a burden on his shoulders. But in spite of Offa's disrespectful words, there was a glint in the old man's eyes that showed that the hoarfrost on his ancient head had not frozen his wits yet.

'Undo that net!' he said.

Cealla and Readda jumped to obey him. They uncorded the net, and then stood back, well out of the way, for they thought the thing was spiteful. For an instant it made no move, and then it unbowed its head, and shook itself free of encumbrance. Slowly the man stood up, uncoiling his cramped limbs, and stretching, and he stood higher and higher, towering over Cealla and Readda, till they fell right back into the crowd, and were amazed at their luck in having caught him. He was a man of great girth, as well as of great height. His wide shoulders were dressed in a mantle of thick fur, and his hair was long, and so dark that the streaks in it showed like silver, shining on his temples and in his close-cropped beard. He stood up, and he looked straight at Arnulf, and he said nothing at all.

'Ah!' said Arnulf at last. 'I never thought to see you again.'

The woodwose returned his stare. Then, 'No man loses an enemy as easily as that,' he said.

'An enemy?' said Arnulf. 'I had forgotten that.'

'*Forgotten?*' cried the other, raising his voice. 'Shall I remind you? Shall I, with all your people listening, remind you what sort of man

54

you are?' He spoke English oddly, on a slightly singing note, like the voice of a slave, but he bore himself all the time more like a king.

'I had forgotten that,' said Arnulf, still softly. 'No feelings burn me now. I am an old tree and the sap no longer wells up into my heart. Each day I think less of the past, and more of what there will be for supper.'

His calm seemed to enrage the woodwose, who clenched his fists till the veins stood out upon the backs of his hands, and ground his heel in the dust as he stood.

'Cast back your mind at least to see how this treatment compares with the welcome I gave you, when I was lord here,' he said. 'Were you beaten and starved as I have been? Or did I give you meat and drink, and a place by the fire in my house, and gold torques to wear upon your arms?'

bracelets made of twisted metal

'You are right, you are right, Dux,' said Arnulf. 'My thanes, bring out a stool for this man, and a horn of ale, and a loaf of bread. Anyone coming from so long ago is welcome to me now, friend and enemy alike.' And with this a steadier note sounded in Arnulf's quavering voice, and men went running to obey him.

'I should not be welcome were I to remind you further,' said the man called Dux, with a kind of grim satisfaction. 'I have long turned over in my mind how little you would have to say for yourself, if I stood face to face with you, and accused you!'

A faint tone of amusement crept into Arnulf's voice. 'You were right, for as you see, I find little to say to you. But you, Dux, say all you like, if words are what you came for.'

But the stool, and the bread, and the ale-horn having now arrived, the Dux sat down, and ate ravenously.

Everyone watched him. Little by little the slaves had put down their work, and come creeping up to stand behind their masters and see and hear with them, so that in Arnulf's kitchen the supper pot was fast boiling dry, and in the field behind Brunhelm's house a lamb bleated piteously in the thorn bush that had caught it, and nobody came.

Sitting down, the woodwose did not look so much bigger than other men, and although he still looked uncommonly black, it seemed shameful to Readda to be afraid of something so piteously hungry; and it occurred to him that he and his neighbours had caught the woodwose, and yet they had not been heard.

He spoke up. 'This stranger should take care how he threatens Arnulf, who is lord here,' he said. 'There is nothing he can tell us that we do not know. We know very well how we came here.'

'Do you then?' asked the Dux, speaking between mouthfuls, and turning upon Readda the fierce gaze of his coal-black eyes.

'Oh yes,' said Readda. 'We have a song about it, that we can all sing.'

'Oh yes,' said Totta, looking round from behind his father's knee. 'It is a good song, very long, and it has Arnulf's name in it, though it is true they sing it in the next valley too, and the way they sing it there, it has nothing about Arnulf at all. . . .' He broke off with a squeak, for his father had clapped a hand over his mouth to stop him, and was shaking him wrathfully.

The stranger's lip curled in visible contempt. But Arnulf was rocking himself to and fro in his chair, his mouth stretched wide in a grin of toothless glee, and laughing a cracked gasping laugh, which quickly made him cough. It took him a long time to get his breath back, and then he said, 'Come, Dux, would you like to hear the song, since you are in it, though not, like me, by name? I am sure Readda here will have his boy sing it to you!' and he rocked with laughter again.

'A harp, bring out a harp!' cried the delighted onlookers, for songs were usually kept for winter evenings, and the chance of entertainment in the middle of the autumn sowing was rare indeed. The crowd moved closer in. A little wooden harp was brought out, and Readda took it, and struck the notes for Totta to sing.

'Listen! we have heard of the glorious deeds
Of our princes, in days of old!'

the childish voice rang clear.

The tune of the song was the same, line after line, as it was the story in the song men listened for. The story told how there had once been a time when this land belonged to Bretmen. Then a great king rose up in a far country, whose thanes were the bravest in the northern lands, and his fame spread far and wide. The Bretmen sent to him for help, because they were greatly afflicted with strong enemies, and they could not win battles. The king sent out his thanes to help them, and many of the famous warriors went into Bretland. The song gave all their names, and Arnulf's name was among them.

As the words of this song rang in his ears, the proud bearing of the Dux slowly changed. He sat in an attitude of terrible sadness, stone-still. The marks of the years upon his face deepened; they could see that he too was an old man; younger than Arnulf by many years, and yet himself with perhaps three-score years behind him. The holiday feeling that the song had brought to the onlookers faded away as they looked at him.

Totta ran out of breath, and faltered, and the harp was passed to Aelward, a lad of nearly twenty, who was Arnulf's great-grandson. But before he struck the guiding notes upon the strings, the Dux spoke up.

'You have left out the tale of your misfortunes, Arnulf. If the song told all that you owed to me, it would make your treason show in its true light! You have left out the glory and the generosity of my people, so that no memory is left of all that you destroyed!'

'The glory of your folk?' said Arnulf. 'That must be one of those things I have forgotten. I remember that they did no work, and had such soft hands that even the hilt of a sword could wound them let alone the blade! I remember that they were so weak-minded they could not remember their own tales, but needed runes upon paper to keep their wordhoards safe. I remember that they lacked strength even to sit upon stools to eat, but lay like sick men, lolling upon couches, wearing white cloaks, and calling themselves citizens, or senators, or some such fooling word, and scorning those who farmed and fought for them!'

The Dux jumped to his feet in anger, and cried out in a strange jumbled tongue that nobody could understand.

'As for the other thing,' continued Arnulf evenly, 'the tale of my misfortunes before I came to you, why, if you think it would make a better song, take the harp, and put it in!' And now the danger in his mild voice could be heard by everyone, and the chill of it held all the onlookers silent.

The Dux said, 'It is not true that you came as a hero whom we asked to come to our aid. You came with scarcely a thread to your back, and with no weapon even at your side, because in your own land there had been a famine, and the people blamed the king for it, and had driven you away. You offered me your skill in battle as payment for the bread you begged from me. And because you were a king, I took pity on you, and gave you lands and a place among my people. And I loved you for your courage, and the grandeur of your ways, and I gave you great gifts, and a ship, and sent you to bring more men like yourself.'

'And so I did, I did,' said Arnulf, but while he spoke he was laughing again, with a savage, cold mirth. 'Will you hear more of the song, that you may add to it?'

'I do not need to hear it,' said the Dux bitterly. 'I can guess how it will go on.' His hearers were disappointed, for the next passage was one they liked, full of battle and blood. 'It will say that you fought battles for us, and won them all. That is true enough. And it will say that I promised you land, and then refused to give it, which is a lie! I gave and gave, and still you wanted more. I gave land till there was none for my own people, and still you brought one man after another, saying he had fought, or his father had fought my battles, and he had no patrimony. You would not be content with any payment, but wanted to inherit all and cast out the true heirs. You wanted to be lords along with us, and bring your barbarous ways into our ancient realm. That is the truth behind your lying song!'

It was clear from the way he looked round him that the Dux expected to be struck down for speaking in this way; but nobody raised a hand against him till Arnulf spoke, and when Arnulf spoke it was still in the same unruffled icy voice.

'No, Dux,' said Arnulf, 'that is not the truth.' And then, with a glitter of triumph in his pale eyes, 'But if you want truth you can have it. The truth is that you wanted something for nothing. You thought we could be kept as dogs are kept for hunting, and cast out of sight and sound when the hunt is over. You thought we would remain poor grateful wanderers, year after year, and you did not reckon on the passing of time. Look round you, Dux, and see. The old men here are my sons and their companions, and then there are my sons' sons, and their grandsons. You did not reckon that we would have sons who would grow up here, knowing no other home, feeling their right like your right, and wanting an equal share in the land they fought for. The truth is that there was no land for our sons, and no shrines for our gods, and so when Aella the great war-lord came over the sea to us, we turned on you and drove you out. He became the Bretwalda, and the king of the South Saxons, and since then the ways of this place have been our ways. Is that enough truth for you, or will you have more? The song does not tell that I was a king in exile when I came to you; you complained of that. Now have the truth instead; I was a convicted thief, fleeing from justice. The rusty sword I inherited from my miserable father was good enough for scaring the folk of lonely farmsteads, and carrying off the handful of coins they kept hidden beneath their floors; it was good for nought else, and soon there was a hue and cry after me. . . .' Arnulf spoke loudly, with wicked joy in his voice, watching the Dux all the time, and not seeing the shock on the faces of his own people.

'. . . so I fled here,' he cried, 'and found that any fool tale would be believed, and any man who was brave enough to rob a farm would seem brave enough to lead an army!'

'The wolf that feeds on corpses is not more vile than you!' said the Dux, and he spoke in a hoarse whisper, as though Arnulf's truth had taken his breath away.

'Am I a king, Dux, a hero?' crowed Arnulf. 'Then it is you who made me one! Perhaps you are right, and I do owe you gratitude!'

The old man's ugly cackling laugh rang loudly in the stunned silence. Then the crowd laughed too; laughed wildly from shock, from disillusion, from delight at his impudence and cunning. All round the Dux their voices hooted in harsh derisive mirth. And there was nothing he could do with his anger. He stood and shook with it from head to foot.

'You had better not have come back, Dux,' said Readda at last, feeling sorry for him.

The woodwose recovered his dignity at once. 'I came to find out what has happened to my people, before I die,' he said.

'It is in the song,' said Arnulf maliciously. 'Sing it to him, Aelward.'

But now they had all had enough of the old man's cruel game. 'Lord Arnulf . . .' said Aelward, protesting.

'*Sing!*' said Arnulf in a terrible voice.

Trembling, Aelward sang. The people listened uneasily, hearing the tale of bloodshed as though for the first time, for the first time as though the names in it were the names of real men. The song told of the wars of Aella and of his victory, and of the place of slaughter, and of the great numbers of Bretmen slain. And after the victory the men of the South Saxons killed all the Bretmen, until none were left alive, and drove them out of the land, and took the great kingdom for themselves. There was no mercy shown to the conquered, but all were killed . . .

A little tremor ran round the circle as Aelward reached the terrible line:

'Because they had been abandoned by their lord.'

The people held their breath, and all looked at the Dux, for it was true that he was still alive, when a brave man would have been dead.

'That is the truth. Take your answer and go,' said Arnulf.

The Dux did not even flinch. 'You murdered them all?' he asked.

'All. And laboured many days to bury them,' said Arnulf savagely.

'There are none of your people here,' said Aelward to the Dux, speaking gently. 'We have never heard of a Bretman in all our valley. They are gone without trace.'

'Without trace?' cried the Dux. 'Look at yourselves!' He turned round to face the crowd which circled him. 'Do you not know the

Saxons were fair; all of them? They had pale hair, and blue eyes. Look at yourselves!'

And men looked at each other, as though seeing for the first time the brown hair, the green and hazel eyes, the dark locks among the fair, and the blazing red of Readda's kin. And among the slaves, heads were even darker, though there too some were fair.

'You are a mongrel pack!' said the Dux, and then turned to Arnulf again. '*Lord*,' he said, framing the word slowly, 'you have honours to match your years, and you see your children and your children's children stand up tall before you. When it comes to a struggle between you and me, you outwit me, as you always did. But now, will you not tell me what happened to my kin, when the great battle was lost for me?'

Then suddenly there was no glee in Arnulf's face, or in his voice. He sounded old and tired. 'Your son we flogged and hanged for calling himself a prince,' he said. 'Your daughter was taken as a bed-slave by Wulfwin, the sword-smith. She had three children, all slaves from the day of their birth. The first died in the year we had a plague of coughing-sickness; the second was hanged to turn away the wrath of Woden, in a year when the harvest was bad. The youngest still lives. He was freed when his master died, and he farms a churl's holding down the valley. If I am not mistaken, he had a hand in catching and beating you.'

For a few moments the Dux stood with bowed head, not moving; and Cealla had time to realize that he himself was the freed-slave of whom Arnulf spoke. He raised a hand to his black hair, bewildered. Arnulf sat blinking the lids of his watery eyes, and his hand lost its grip on the arm of his chair, and wandered, shaking. If he was thinking of anything at all now, it was probably of his supper.

Then the Dux turned round. He looked searchingly at Cealla. All eyes looked with him, and Cealla shrank from them. He was not used to getting much attention.

'Come away with me, grandson, and be a prince, as your royal blood entitles you,' said the Dux grandly. 'I have a kingdom still to defend, and a caister to defend it from. You shall lead a band of brave warriors, and be called their lord. Will you come?'

Cealla looked down, away from the dark blazing eyes. 'I have my corn to plant,' he said unhappily. Then, cheering up a little, he added, 'But it is not the way of our folk to turn their backs on their kin. If you are kin of mine, come home with me, and there shall always be a stool beside the hearth for you, and a ladle from the stew-pot for your bowl.'

'The slave-iron bit deep into your heart, that you can make such an offer to me, to a king!' cried the Dux.

'Were you to work in the fields, and hunt in the forest for the food and fire you live by, you would not think so little of them!' cried Cealla, angered, and speaking proudly.

And looking at Cealla's angry face, the Dux smiled, suddenly, a smile that quickly turned into bitter self-mockery. 'No,' he said. 'I will go back to my patch of hill-rock and heather, and my half-dozen tattered men, and be a king there alone. But you are still my heir, entitled to all I have left. Take your inheritance!' And he put into Cealla's hand a small disk of coppery silver.

Cealla looked at it, and found it was a coin. He had never held one before, though he had seen one which Arnulf had, and proudly showed round. The coin had rune-writing round a man's head. MAXIMIAN DUX. Cealla could not read it.

'Thank you,' he said, turning the coin over and over. 'Perhaps this will bring a better husband for my girl, when the time comes for her to marry.'

But the Dux had turned and gone at once, and was striding away up the hillside to the top of the valley.

Running some way behind him went Wulfrun. She must have been hiding somewhere all this time, and she cried after him, 'Wood-wose, woodwose, they are going to burn down the wood this winter to make a new field, and then where will you go?'

He neither stopped, nor turned his head.

'Oh, woodwose,' cried the child's voice, shaking with tears, 'there will be no wild for you to hide in, nowhere for you to go!'

But he was already out of sight among the trees. Clutching his penny, Cealla started up the hill to fetch his daughter and dry her tears. A slave-woman poured water in the pot to save Arnulf's burnt supper, and someone set free the bleating lamb.

JILL PATON WALSH

The Harpooning

Where the seas are open moor
and level blue, limitless,
and swells are as soft grasses
rolling over with the wind,
often to the idleness
of Azorean summer

come the great whales. Long granites
grow, slowly awash with sun,
and waves lap along black skin
cleansing | like the shine of a laving
rain upon a city pavement.
Together they come, yet alone

they seem to lie. Massively
still, they bask, breathing like men.
Silent among them there is one
so huge he enters the eye
whole, leaving the rest unseen.
His sons and cows idly

loll, as if in wait. Inside
him, too, tethered now, there waits
the bulk and strength of a herd
of a dozen rogue elephant;
they strain taut thongs of his will,
laziness | and paw against such indolence.

Anger, could snap them loose –
anger, or hunger. Jungles
under a mile of ocean,
where no light has ever been,
would splinter, and the blind squid
uncoil in him like oily trees.

But the squint jaws close on bone
steady as a castle door-jamb;
and, bigger than a drawbridge,
his tail flukes are calm upon
the calmer water. While the sun
still pleases him, he will grudge

himself no pleasure. He blows
old air from his lungs, cones
rising whitely. Through the hard,
final coursings of his blood
the oars will not rouse him. Thick
blubber houses him like hot meringue.

TED WALKER

Kamik, His Companions Killed, Struggles Back to His Camp

Kamik knows the storm is coming. The wind is rising stronger every hour. The cold arctic wind blows in his face, but he doesn't care. He is hot and welcomes the cold wind. He can see the first sight of dawn. He has walked all night. If a storm does come, it will help him, for no wild animal travels when there is a storm. At least he will be safe from animals if a storm comes. By the time the sun is high, the snow is blowing and getting worse. Kamik shields his face with his hands to keep off the snow. With little hope for survival, he goes on. At least this time nature is on his side.

The storm has grown worse, but Kamik goes on. He can see only a few steps ahead. Knowing wild animals will not travel in this storm makes him feel safe. But the wind itself is slowing him up, and he has to fight it hard each time he takes a step. He doesn't know just what is ahead, but he knows that if he keeps heading into the wind he is heading in the right direction. Sometimes he has to stop and wipe the snow off his face. The small store of meat on his back seems to weigh a hundred seals, but the meat is the most precious treasure he has now. Without food he won't survive another night. The snow is soft and makes travelling hard. He knows he must travel as far as possible each day if he is to make home. He wants to see his mother. This gives him the will to live.

Kamik falls to the ground heavily and doesn't bother to get up. His lungs are burning. The snow builds up around his body. He knows that if he stays like this he will be buried in a few minutes. He forces himself to get up. He knows that he has to make a small igloo to spend the night in. He finds a good place to make one. A few minutes later he is struggling to put one block of snow on top of another. Each block seems heavier than the previous one. As he works slowly, the snow keeps falling on his face. It feels good, for he is sweating. After he has completed the igloo he goes inside. It is dark, but at least there is no wind. In darkness he chews a frozen piece of seal meat. It tastes good. After he has eaten, he spreads a small sealskin and lies down on it and tries to go to sleep.

He hears a voice calling him, 'Kamik, Kamik!' With a start he suddenly sits up. Then he realizes that it was only a dream. He has wakened in a cold sweat, the voice sounded so real. His heart beats faster and faster. Is the spirit of the dead trying to call him? There he lies, his eyes wide open in fear.

He doesn't know how he got back to sleep, but when he opens his eyes again the igloo is no longer dark. He gets up and goes outside. The wind is still blowing strong, but the storm has passed. He goes to the top of an ice ridge and looks all round. He can see the mountains far away, maybe three sunrises away. He decides he will head for those mountains, but once near them he must stay and travel on ice. He knows there is more danger on land than there is on sea. Wolves and musk oxen roam the land, living on anything they can kill. Wolves will not attack a man unless he is sleeping, but the musk ox is different. Kamik goes down from the top of the ridge and goes inside his igloo. He has a small piece of meat. Shortly he starts to walk again. He wonders. Will this be his last day? He isn't sure that he will stay alive long enough to see another sunrise.

Tired as he is, Kamik doesn't dare rest. He knows each mile brings higher hope for survival. He is sweating, the little sack on his back seems to weigh a hundred seals. The knife he is holding seems to try to force him to fall. Each time he takes a step, his feet refuse to move as quickly as he commands. His lungs are burning and his heart is beating like a sealskin drum. Still he forces every part of his body to move. While day is here, he must go on until his command is refused.

Darkness comes slowly as Kamik moves on. He wants to stop and rest, but he keeps saying to himself that he must move on while there is a little daylight. So far he has been lucky. Another day is almost past and he is still alive. Soon he will stop and make an igloo for the night.

When darkness comes he can go on no longer. He drops to the snow and rests. Slowly his body begins to relax. He doesn't want to get up again but forces himself to start looking around for a place to build a small igloo. He finds a good spot, and soon he is struggling to put one snow block upon another. It seems a long time later that he at last completes his construction. Once inside, he takes out a small piece of meat and chews on it hungrily. He can feel the cold frozen meat as it settles in his stomach. He forces himself to stop while there is a small piece of it left. This meat is his hope for survival before starving to death. By his side is his harpoon, which can mean life or death. The harpoon, which is so small, yet holds such power.

After he has put the small piece of meat in his sack, Kamik puts some snow in his mouth and melts it. When it has melted, he washes his hands with it and drinks what is left. He wipes his hands on his

sealskin pants and lies down. He tries to close his eyes to sleep, but sleep will not come. Now he can do no more, only wait for to-morrow.

Another day comes for Kamik. Once again he is ready. His muscles are sore from the previous day, but he tries not to think about it. No matter where the pain comes from, he must fight it; this is the only way to reach home. There is a strong wind blowing, but still he is hot as he walks. He wishes he was cold instead, for when a man is cold he can walk faster and easier. He rubs some snow on his face and it immediately melts against his warm cheek. Much later he comes to the rough ice. This will make it much tougher than smooth ice, and it will tear his caribou skin boots more quickly. Still he must go through it, to go around would waste many hours. He knows that before he reaches home he will be almost barefoot, his boots will be spent. With the soles gone he will be exposed to the snow, and frostbite will come. He knows how it feels to have frostbitten feet. But there are many things to worry about before that time comes. He knows he can run into trouble any minute from now.

Kamik has travelled far. The ice he is walking on is rough, and already he can see that the soles of his boots are beginning to tear. he can see the mountains clearly now, but they are still maybe two sunrises away. And he only hopes he will not see bear on the way. He is hungry, but he doesn't dare eat what he has left. The meat he is carrying is too small. He plans to eat it at sunset time. He doesn't dare stop and look for seal holes. This would take too much time. His feet feel pain as he steps on a sharp piece of ice, but at least they are warm. He knows that as soon as he stops walking he will feel cold. He feels so tired and so hungry that he almost wishes he were dead. But no, he mustn't talk or think like that. He is suffering to live. Death comes easy, and he must fight to live. He has lived through many deaths and walked away; he must reach home. He is so deep in thought that he doesn't try to get up, but lies with tears rolling down his cheeks. For a long time he doesn't move. He looks at his harpoon lying a few steps from him. He takes it in his hands and stares at it for a long time. Kneeling in the snow, he slowly puts the sharp tip of the harpoon to his throat. One move and he will suffer no more. Quickly he throws it down and once again falls to the snow, crying loudly.

A long time later he sits up, staring sightlessly at the sky. 'Taking my own life will not change things,' he says to himself. 'A good hunter does not give up easily. I must control my madness.' He thinks how his mother would feel. And once again he falls down and cries.

Night comes and he can no longer go on. He is starting to build his igloo when a thought strikes him. Maybe he has a better chance travelling by night than by day. Surely if he can't see the animals because of darkness, then animals can't see him either. One thing, though. Animals smell without seeing, and he doesn't. He will have to take chances. Travelling by night is a good idea, but he will have to sleep very little. He decides he must take the chance. He stops cutting snow, takes out his meat, and chews on it. This is the last meat. He eats all of it. Now he is facing death by starvation as well. He must plan.

He decides he must hunt. This will slow him, but he has no choice. Without food he will starve. He must hunt during the day and sleep little. If he gets food, he will continue towards home at night. He decides to hunt near land when he gets there. If he doesn't get food from the sea, he will hunt on land for musk ox, wolves, ptarmigans – anything, even lemmings. He will hunt near those mountains. If he fails to get food, he will choose to die there. With this plan in mind, he walks on into the night.

When Kamik opens his eyes it is dark. He has slept too long and night has come. His little caribou skin offers small protection from the cold air. He rises slowly and stretches; his muscles are sore. But he must start again. Another night and he is sure he will reach the mountains. That will be the place to start hunting for food.

The lone figure moves slowly. He travels in darkness, never sure what lies ahead. The snow he is walking on is hard and hurts his feet. His feet are beginning to feel cold, the soles of his boots are torn. Even in darkness he can see the mountains ahead. Today he must get food or he will grow weak from hunger; and he knows he must be strong to survive. He decides he will hunt before going to sleep again. He will hunt in the daytime and sleep at night. He is thankful that this is the last night in which he will have to travel. Once at his destination, he will hunt until he gets food or until starvation comes.

He is exhausted by the time first daylight appears on the horizon. He has walked all night without rest, but his endless walk has been rewarded. Now his destination is close. From here on he will look for seal holes. Much later, he finds a good seal hole. He waits until his feet can't stand the feel of cold snow. He has to stop watching and walk for a while. When his feet get warmer, he goes back to the seal hole again and waits. Now darkness comes close again, and still no food. He is weak now. No food and too much travel have begun to take their toll. He can feel the first signs of starvation. Darkness comes and he begins to build an igloo. This will be his home until he gets food and can go on, or until death comes. When he has completed his igloo, he sits inside. It is dark and cold. The only possessions he has now are his harpoon, his ivory knife, a sealskin rope, his sealskin sack.

A sealskin sack!

A sealskin sack is food. He has been carrying food all along and didn't know it. His sack is dry, but it is food. 'He told me once that when you're facing starvation anything made of animal can be eaten,' he thinks, remembering his father's words. 'My sack, my rope, my clothes and caribou hide are all food.' He takes his knife and picks up his rope. Tonight he will eat it. Tomorrow he can eat what's left of it. When that is gone he will start on his sack. This will give him a hope of surviving until he can kill an animal. He chews on the rope wildly. It is tasteless, still it is food. It makes him feel better in the stomach.

Still more surprises.

His sack and caribou hide! He can tear his caribou hide and make himself soles for his boots. He will use the rope and wrap the hide around his feet. With these thoughts, he smiles. The clothing he wears will be his food as well. With better hope he lies down, and sleep comes instantly.

With the sun shining brightly in a cloudless sky, Kamik comes out of his small igloo. He looks around. The wind is calm; this will be a good day to hunt for seals. He goes back inside and takes his sealskin rope. He takes his knife and cuts the rope into small pieces. This done, he chews on the rope hungrily. After he has eaten, he goes out again with his harpoon and his knife in his hands. He looks up to the great cliff. It is high, like trying to reach heaven. The cliff is straight up. To get to the top, he will have to go around to the other side. But that will be another day. Today he will hunt seals in the sea. If he fails to get food, he will hunt on the land next. Some time later he finds a seal hole. It is good, and his hopes are now higher. He begins his first wait. He must be patient; he knows that in everyone's life patience is important.

Darkness comes again. Kamik has waited all day and no seal has come. He is tired and hungry. He knows that tonight he will have to eat sealskin rope again. He decides that tomorrow he will hunt on the land. He is weak and he starts back towards his small igloo.

The first ray of the sun is hitting the sky as Kamik goes out. He is hungry and cold, but at least he has had a good night's sleep. He starts towards the mountain, to its right side. He can see that the cliff is lower on that side. He knows that it will take a lot of strength, something he doesn't have now, but he has no choice but to climb. The land is his last hope. The edge of the cliff is rocky and it hurts his feet. Still he struggles. He looks down to where he was at sunrise. He is high, and he knows that if he slips he will roll and never stop until he gets to the bottom. He knows he will die before reaching the bottom.

The sun is high by the time he gets to the top. He is sweating and out of breath; he lies still for a long time. Wiping the sweat from his face, he feels better. As he gets slowly to his feet, he gets a shock. The howling sound of wolves – and close. Holding his harpoon tightly in his hands, he goes towards a rock. When he reaches the rock he looks over it and his eyes open wide. He sees three wolves attacking four musk oxen, the wolves howling as they start towards the musk oxen, which have formed a circle to protect their young one. One bull gets out of the circle and charges at one wolf. The wolf dodges and the musk ox misses its mark. Kamik knows musk oxen are helpless against such foes. He knows wolves don't fear animals. They fear man.

'They fear a man,' Kamik thinks. He looks back where he has just come from. Then a thought strikes him. It is dangerous, but then again he has been in danger for so long that it makes no difference. He suddenly exposes himself to the wolves and musk oxen. With a yell, and waving his arms wildly, he goes towards the beasts. The wolves stop their.attack and look at him. Seeing the man, the wolves leap and are off. The musk oxen stay in their circle unmoving. Now it is time to proceed to his plan. Yelling loudly, Kamik goes towards the circle of musk oxen. He knows that sooner or later the bull will charge him. This is part of his plan. Now he is close enough to hurl his harpoon. He knows that one strike will never kill a musk ox, but with all his might he hurls the harpoon. It goes straight and fast towards the bull. The harpoon strikes the beast on its side. Now Kamik is sure the bull will charge. The big beast jumps and charges at Kamik. Kamik runs towards the cliff with the beast a few steps away.

Will his plan work, or will the bull get to him before he reaches the edge of the cliff?

Kamik gets to the edge and turns. He sees the beast charging at him at full speed. When the bull is only a few steps away, Kamik steps aside and lies flat on the snow. The bull, with the harpoon in its side, doesn't stop. Too late, the beast sees the cliff and tries to stop, but it is going too fast. It falls over the cliff to certain death. Kamik's plan has worked. Now all he has to do is climb down to the dead animal and eat. Climbing down is not easy, with every chance to slide down and die. But with food waiting at the bottom, Kamik goes down without thinking of danger. At the bottom, he finds the dead animal. At once he starts cutting. After he has cut the animal, he eats wildly and licks at its blood. It is good. Now he has every chance to get food, and takes all he can eat. Now he has food for many sunrises. Maybe he will get home after all.

He gets back to his igloo at sunset. He carries a heavy load of meat on his back. After he has put all the meat away, he lies down. he feels sick. He knows why he is sick. After too many days without food, he has eaten too much. He hopes the sickness will be gone by morning.

Kamik has travelled all day without rest. He hasn't got far, but he has gained another day without danger, and he is tired as he lies in his igloo. It has been a hard day, maybe harder than any other day he has travelled. The meat he carried was heavy. It was hot, without wind. The night has come too soon for him. He is tired and needs rest, but he had wanted to get farther than he is now. The longer he travels the closer he will get to home. For a long time, sleep doesn't come. He keeps listening for a sound. 'The sound of what?' he asks himself. Maybe he is listening for the sound of dogs and people, or maybe for the sound of the steps of a bear. The thought of a bear

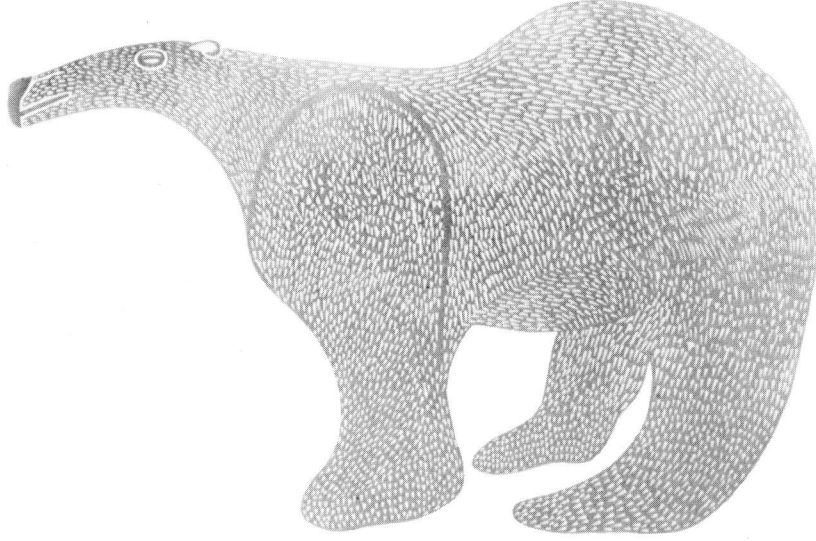

coming scares him. For a long time sleep doesn't come, and when he finally goes to sleep he begins to re-live in his dream the day his friend was killed. In his dream he sees himself and young Soonah battling the bear. Suddenly he wakes up with a scream. He is sweating. Then he realizes it is only a dream. He listens for a sound and none comes. He lies with fear in his eyes, and sleep will not come.

The load he is carrying forces Kamik to stop and rest. He takes the load off his back and sits on the ice. Just as he starts to lie on his back, he hears a roar. Kamik jumps to his feet and turns. He sees a bear. He takes his harpoon and runs to the top of a large ice ridge. Here, he decides, he will make his stand to the end. Kamik is surprised that the bear does not go after him. Instead it goes to his meat and eats hungrily. Kamik watches the bear with fear. He knows that as soon as it has eaten his meat it will go after him. The great animal finishes the meat quickly and then turns to look at Kamik. Kamik knows this is the moment. The bear walks slowly towards Kamik and stops. He knows the bear is sure it will have another meal soon and is taking its time attacking the hunter. Kamik waits, holding the harpoon tightly, as the bear starts again slowly towards him. He holds his harpoon tightly between himself and the bear. He is high enough so that the bear will have to stand on its hind legs to touch him.

The bear roars and charges at full speed. Once reaching Kamik, it takes a slash at him with its powerful paw. Kamik holds his ground and the bear strikes the sharp end of his harpoon. Its leg cut and in pain, the bear roars in pain and goes to the ground. Kamik can see the blood, but he knows that a single cut like that will never kill the bear. The bear gets on its hind legs again and tries to jump at Kamik. Kamik holds his harpoon, and the bear runs into it, and the harpoon cuts the bear on its shoulder. The blood comes.

Kamik grows tired and hot. His head throbs and his muscles are sore. He knows the bear can tire him out if he doesn't kill it fast. But killing a bear fast is impossible with only one harpoon. The bear comes at Kamik blindly and the harpoon cuts its forehead. Kamik sees blood all over, and hope comes. He thinks maybe if he is lucky he will kill the bear in time. Once again the bear charges at full speed. Kamik braces himself and holds the harpoon tightly. The bear jumps, and Kamik thrusts the harpoon towards the bear's neck without letting it go. The harpoon finds its mark and goes deep inside the bear's neck. Not wanting to lose his harpoon, Kamik holds onto it. The bear turns and hits Kamik on his side. Kamik goes flying down. He lands on his back heavily. He gets up in time to see the bear turn towards him. Now he is defenceless.

He sees the bear with his harpoon stuck in its neck. Then he thinks of his knife. He runs towards his knife which he had left beside the meat the bear had eaten. Not daring to look back, he dives for the knife. He gets it in his hand and turns. He sees the bear coming towards him slowly. Now on the ground, and with only a knife in his hands, Kamik knows the end has come. The bear comes slowly. Kamik steps back with hands spread wide, bracing for the fight to the last breath.

Suddenly many sounds come.

Kamik and the bear turn towards the noise at the same time. They both see dogs and men, coming fast. Men with harpoons and the dogs growling. Kamik has been found.

The bear saw its hope die. It turned and tried to run away from the dogs and harpoons, too late. The dogs came in hundreds, biting, howling. Right behind the dogs came men with expert knowledge of how to kill. The harpoons flew and struck. The bear went down.

Kamik fell to the ground breathless. He looked up and saw his mother. Ooramik ran towards him with tears of joy. Kamik got up and received his mother. For a long time they held each other with tears of happiness. For a long time no one spoke.

MARKOOSIE, *Harpoon of the Hunter*

The Castaway

The man on the raft had only hope to keep him alive now. The bones showed through his thin face. An endless moan escaped his trembling mouth. His eyes were bright with fever. He had been clinging to life for more than a month now on this wretched collection of planks.

All at once a new sound reached his enfeebled brain: a buzzing noise imagined in his delirium no doubt. But it wasn't – it really was a helicopter approaching slowly, flying over the raft. Saved! He was saved! The castaway danced about clumsily.

In the meantime a rope-ladder had been lowered from the helicopter. A man dressed in rags, his emaciated face overgrown with a coarse beard, was pushed brutally on to the top rungs.

The helicopter turned away and disappeared.

Now there were two castaways on the raft.

ROLAND TOPOR
Translated from the French by Margaret Crosland and David Le Vay

John Glashan

The Colt

It was the swift coming of spring that let things happen. It was spring, and the opening of the roads, that took his father out of town. It was spring that clogged the river with floodwater and ice floes pans, sent the dogs racing in wild aimless packs, ripped the railroad bridge out and scattered it down the river for exuberant towns-people to fish out piecemeal. It was spring that drove the whole town long hooked poles to the riverbank with pike poles and coffeepots and boxes of sand-wiches for an impromptu picnic, lifting their sober responsibilities Canadian Pacific Railroad out of them and making them whoop blessings on the CPR for a winter's firewood. Nothing might have gone wrong except for the coming of spring. Some of the neighbours might have noticed and let them know; Bruce might not have forgotten; his mother might have remembered and sent him out again after dark.

But the spring came, and the ice went out, and that night Bruce went to bed drunk and exhausted with excitement. In the restless sleep just before waking he dreamed of wolves and wild hunts, but when he awoke finally he realized that he had not been dreaming the noise. The window, wide open for the first time in months, let in a shivery draught of fresh, damp air, and he heard the faint yelping far down in the bend of the river.

He dressed and went downstairs, crowding his bottom into the warm oven, not because he was cold but because it had been a ritual for so long that not even the sight of the sun outside could convince him it wasn't necessary. The dogs were still yapping; he heard them through the open door.

'What's the matter with all the pooches?' he said. 'Where's Spot?'

'He's out with them,' his mother said. 'They've probably got a porcupine treed. Dogs go crazy in the spring.'

'It's dog days they go crazy.'

'They go crazy in the spring, too.' She hummed a little as she set the table. 'You'd better go feed the horses. Breakfast won't be for ten minutes. And see if Daisy is all right.'

Bruce stood perfectly still in the middle of the kitchen. 'Oh, my gosh!' he said. 'I left Daisy picketed out all night!'

His mother's head jerked around. 'Where?'

'Down in the bend.'

'Where those dogs are?'

'Yes,' he said, sick and afraid. 'Maybe she's had her colt.'

'She couldn't for two or three days,' his mother said. But just looking at her he knew that it might be bad, that there was something to be afraid of. In another moment they were both out the door, both running.

But it couldn't be Daisy they were barking at, he thought as he raced around Chance's barn. He'd picketed her higher up, not clear down in the U where the dogs were. His eyes swept the brown, wet, close-cropped meadow, the edge of the brush where the river ran

slope close under the north bench. The mare wasn't there! He opened his mouth and half turned, running, to shout at his mother coming behind him, and then sprinted for the deep curve of the bend.

As soon as he rounded the little clump of brush that fringed the cut-bank behind Chance's he saw them. The mare stood planted, a bay spot, against the grey brush, and in front of her, on the ground, was another smaller spot. Six or eight dogs were leaping around, barking, sitting. Even at that distance he recognized Spot and the Chapmans' airedale.

He shouted and pumped on. At a gravelly patch he stooped and clawed and straightened, still running, with a handful of pebbles. In one pausing, straddling, aiming motion he let fly a rock at the distant pack. It fell far short, but they turned their heads, sat on their haunches and let out defiant short barks. Their tongues lolled as if they had run far.

Bruce yelled and threw again, one eye on the dogs and the other on the chestnut colt in front of the mare's feet. The mare's ears were back, and as he ran, Bruce saw the colt's head bob up and down. It was all right then. The colt was alive. He slowed and came up quietly. Never move fast or speak loud around an animal, Pa said.

The colt struggled again, raised its head with white eyeballs rolling, spraddled its white-stockinged legs and tried to stand. 'Easy, boy,' Bruce said. 'Take it easy, old fella.' His mother arrived, getting her breath, her hair half down, and he turned to her gleefully. 'It's all right, Ma. They didn't hurt anything. Isn't he a beauty, Ma?'

He stroked Daisy's nose. She was heaving, her ears pricking forward and back; her flanks were lathered, and she trembled. Patting her gently, he watched the colt, sitting now like a dog on its haunches, and his happiness that nothing had really been hurt bubbled out of him. 'Lookit, Ma,' he said. 'He's got four white socks. Can I call him Socks, Ma? He sure is a nice colt, isn't he? Aren't you, Socks, old boy?' He reached down to touch the chestnut's forelock, and the colt struggled, pulling away.

Then Bruce saw his mother's face. It was quiet, too quiet. She hadn't answered a word to all his jabber. Instead she knelt down, about ten feet from the squatting colt, and stared at it. The boy's eyes followed hers. There was something funny about . . .

'Ma!' he said. 'What's the matter with its front feet?'

He left Daisy's head and came around, staring. The colt's pasterns looked bent – *were* bent, so that they flattened clear to the ground under its weight. Frightened by Bruce's movement, the chestnut flopped and floundered to its feet, pressing close to its mother. As it walked, Bruce saw, flat on its fetlocks, its hooves sticking out in front like a movie comedian's too-large shoes.

Bruce's mother pressed her lips together, shaking her head. She moved so gently that she got her hand on the colt's poll, and he bobbed against the pleasant scratching. 'You poor broken-legged thing,' she said with tears in her eyes. 'You poor little friendly ruined thing!'

Still quietly, she turned towards the dogs, and for the first time in his life Bruce heard her curse. Quietly, almost in a whisper, she cursed them as they sat with hanging tongues just out of reach. 'God damn you,' she said. 'God damn your wild hearts, chasing a mother and a poor little colt.'

To Bruce, standing with trembling lips, she said, 'Go get Jim Enich. Tell him to bring a wagon. And don't cry. It's not your fault.'

His mouth tightened; a sob jerked in his chest. He bit his lip and drew his face down tight to keep from crying, but his eyes filled and ran over.

'It is too my fault!' he said, and turned and ran.

Later, as they came in the wagon up along the cutbank, the colt tied down in the wagon box with his head sometimes lifting, sometimes bumping on the boards, the mare trotting after with chuckling vibrations of solicitude in her throat, Bruce leaned far over and tried to touch the colt's haunch. 'Gee whiz!' he said. 'Poor old Socks.'

His mother's arm was around him, keeping him from leaning over too far. He didn't watch where they were until he heard his mother say in surprise and relief, 'Why, there's Pa!'

Instantly he was terrified. He had forgotten and left Daisy staked out all night. It was his fault, the whole thing. He slid back into the seat and crouched between Enich and his mother, watching from that narrow space like a gopher from its hole. He saw the Ford against the barn and his father's big body leaning into it and pulling out gunny sacks and straw. There was mud all over the car, mud on his father's pants. He crouched deeper into his crevice and watched his father's face while his mother was telling what had happened.

Then Pa and Jim Enich lifted and slid the colt down to the ground, and Pa stooped to feel its fetlocks. His face was still, red

burrowing rodent

jute

from wind-burn, and his big square hands were muddy. After a long examination he straightened up.

'Would've been a nice colt,' he said. 'Damn a pack of mangy mongrels, anyway.' He brushed his pants and looked at Bruce's mother. 'How come Daisy was out?'

'I told Brucie to take her out. The Barn seems so cramped for her, and I thought it would do her good to stretch her legs. And then the ice went out, and the bridge with it, and there was a lot of excitement. . . .' She spoke very fast, and in her voice Bruce heard the echo of his own fear and guilt. She was trying to protect him, but in his own mind he knew he was to blame.

'I didn't mean to leave her out, Pa,' he said. His voice squeaked, and he swallowed. 'I was going to bring her in before supper, only when the bridge . . .'

His father's sombre eyes rested on him, and he stopped. But his father didn't fly into a rage. He just seemed tired. He looked at the colt and then at Enich. 'Total loss?' he said.

Enich had a leathery, withered face, with two deep creases from beside his nose to the corner of his mouth. A brown mole hid in the left one, and it emerged and disappeared as he chewed a dry grass stem. 'Hide,' he said.

Bruce closed his dry mouth, swallowed. 'Pa!' he said. 'It won't have to be shot, will it?'

'What else can you do with it?' his father said. 'A crippled horse is no good. It's just plain mercy to shoot it.'

'Give it to me, Pa. I'll keep it lying down and heal it up.'

'Yeah,' his father said, without sarcasm and without mirth. 'You could keep it lying down about one hour.'

Bruce's mother came up next to him, as if the two of them were standing against the others. 'Jim,' she said quickly, 'isn't there some kind of brace you could put on it. I remember my dad had a horse once that broke a leg below the knee, and he saved it that way.'

'Not much chance,' Enich said. 'Both legs, like that.' He plucked a weed and stripped the dry branches from the stalk. 'You can't make a horse understand he has to keep still.'

'But wouldn't it be worth trying?' she said. 'Children's bones heal so fast, I should think a colt's would too.'

'I don't know. There's an outside chance, maybe.'

'Bo,' she said to her husband, 'why don't we try it? It seems such a shame, a lovely colt like that.'

'I know it's a shame!' he said. 'I don't like shooting colts any better than you do. But I never saw a broken-legged colt get well.

It'd just be a lot of worry and trouble, and then you'd have to shoot it finally anyway.'

'Please,' she said. She nodded at him slightly, and then the eyes of both were on Bruce. He felt the tears coming up again, and turned to grope for the colt's ears. It tried to struggle to its feet, and Enich put his foot on its neck. The mare chuckled anxiously.

'How much this hobble brace kind of thing cost?' the father said finally. Bruce turned again, his mouth open with hope.

'Two-three dollars is all,' Enich said.

'You think it's got a chance?'

'One in a thousand, maybe.'

'All right. Let's go see MacDonald.'

'Oh, good!' Bruce's mother said, and put her arm around him tight.

'I don't know whether it's good or not,' the father said. 'We might wish we never did it.' To Bruce he said, 'It's your responsibility. You got to take complete care of it.'

'I will!' Bruce said. He took his hand out of his pocket and rubbed below his eye with his knuckles. 'I'll take care of it every day.'

Big with contrition and shame and gratitude and the sudden sense of immense responsibility, he watched his father and Enich start for the house to get a tape measure. When they were thirty feet away he said loudly, 'Thanks, Pa. Thanks an awful lot.'

His father half-turned, said something to Enich. Bruce stooped to stroke the colt, looked at his mother, started to laugh and felt it turn horribly into a sob. When he turned away so that his mother wouldn't notice he saw his dog Spot looking inquiringly around the corner of the barn. Spot took three or four tentative steps and paused, wagging his tail. Very slowly (never speak loud or move fast around an animal) the boy bent and found a good-sized stone. He straightened casually, brought his arm back, and threw with all his might. The rock caught Spot squarely in the ribs. He yiped, tucked his tail, and scuttled around the barn, and Bruce chased him, throwing clods and stones and gravel, yelling, 'Get out! Go on, get out of here or I'll kick you apart. Get out! Go on!'

So all that spring, while the world dried in the sun and the willows
floodwater stream
emerged from the floodwater and the mud left by the freshet hardened and caked among their roots, and the grass of the meadow greened and the river brush grew misty with tiny leaves and the dandelions spread yellow along the flats, Bruce tended his colt. While the other boys roamed the bench hills with ·22s looking for

gophers or rabbits or sage hens, he anxiously superintended the colt's nursing and watched it learn to nibble the grass. While his gang built a darkly secret hideout in the deep brush beyond Hazards', he was currying and brushing and trimming the chestnut mane. When packs of boys ran hare and hounds through the town and around the river's slow bends, he perched on the front porch with his slingshot and a can full of small round stones, waiting for stray dogs to appear. He waged a holy war on the dogs until they learned to detour widely around his house, and he never did completely forgive his own dog, Spot. His whole life was wrapped up in the hobbled, leg-ironed chestnut colt with the slow-motion lunging walk and the affectionate nibbling lips.

Every week or so Enich, who was now working out of town at the Half Diamond Bar, rode in and stopped. Always, with that expressionless quiet that was terrible to the boy, he stood and looked the colt over, bent to feel pastern and fetlock, stood back to watch the plunging walk when the boy held out a handful of grass. His expression said nothing; whatever he thought was hidden back of his leathery face as the dark mole was hidden in the crease beside his mouth. Bruce found himself watching that mole sometimes, as if revelation might lie there. But when he pressed Enich to tell him, when he said, 'He's getting better, isn't he? He walks better, doesn't he, Mr Enich? His ankles don't bend so much, do they?' the wrangler gave him little encouragement.

'Let him be a while. He's growin', sure enough. Maybe give him another month.'

May passed. The river was slow and clear again, and some of the boys were already swimming. School was almost over. And still Bruce paid attention to nothing but Socks. He willed so strongly that the colt should get well that he grew furious even at Daisy when she sometimes wouldn't let the colt suck as much as he wanted. He took a butcher knife and cut the long tender grass in the fence corners, where Socks could not reach, and fed it to his pet by the handful. He trained him to nuzzle for sugar-lumps in his pockets. And back in his mind was a fear: in the middle of June they would be going out to the homestead again, and if Socks weren't well by that time he might not be able to go.

'Pa,' he said, a week before they planned to leave. 'How much of a load are we going to have, going out to the homestead?'

'I don't know, wagonful, I suppose. Why?'

'I just wondered.' He ran his fingers in a walking motion along the round edge of the dining table, and strayed into the other room. If they had a wagonload, then there was no way Socks could be

combing

horse specialist

loaded in and taken along. And he couldn't walk thirty miles. He'd get left behind before they got up on the bench, hobbling along like the little crippled boy in the Pied Piper, and they'd look back and see him trying to run, trying to keep up.

That picture was so painful that he cried over it in bed that night. But in the morning he dared to ask his father if they couldn't take Socks along to the farm. His father turned on him eyes as sober as Jim Enich's, and when he spoke it was with a kind of tired impatience. 'How can he go? He couldn't walk it.'

'But I want him to go, Pa!'

'Bruce,' his mother said, 'don't get your hopes up. You know we'd do it if we could, if it was possible.'

'But, Ma . . .'

His father said, 'What you want us to do, haul a broken-legged colt thirty miles?'

'He'd be well by the end of the summer, and he could walk back.'

'Look,' his father said. 'Why can't you make up your mind to it? He isn't getting well. He isn't going to get well.'

'He is too getting well!' Bruce shouted. He half stood up at the table, and his father looked at his mother and shrugged.

'Please, Bo,' she said.

'Well, he's got to make up his mind to it sometime,' he said.

Jim Enich's wagon pulled up on Saturday morning, and Bruce was out the door before his father could rise from his chair. 'Hi, Mr Enich,' he said.

'Hello, Bub. How's your pony?'

'He's fine,' Bruce said. 'I think he's got a lot better since you saw him last.'

whip handle 'Uh-huh.' Enich wrapped the lines around the whipstock and climbed down. 'Tell me you're leaving next week.'

'Yes,' Bruce said. 'Socks is in the back.'

When they got into the back yard Bruce's father was there with his hands behind his back, studying the colt as it hobbled around. He looked at Enich. 'What do you think?' he said. 'The kid here thinks his colt can walk out to the homestead.'

'Uh-huh,' Enich said. 'Well, I wouldn't say that.' He inspected the chestnut, scratched between his ears. Socks bobbed, and snuffed at his pockets. 'Kid's made quite a pet of him.'

Bruce's father grunted. 'That's just the damned trouble.'

'I didn't think he could walk out,' Bruce said. 'I thought we could take him in the wagon, and then he'd be well enough to walk back in the fall.'

'Uh,' Enich said. 'Let's take his braces off for a minute.'

He unbuckled the triple straps on each leg, pulled the braces off, and stood back. The colt stood almost as flat on his fetlocks as he had the morning he was born. Even Bruce, watching with his whole mind tight and apprehensive, could see that. Enich shook his head.

'You see, Bruce?' his father said. 'It's too bad, but he isn't getting better. You'll have to make up your mind. . . .'

'He will get better though!' Bruce said. 'It just takes a long time is all.' He looked at his father's face, at Enich's, and neither one had any hope in it. But when Bruce opened his mouth to say something else his father's eyebrows drew down in sudden, uncontrollable anger, and his hand made an impatient sawing motion in the air.

'We shouldn't have tried this in the first place,' he said. 'It just tangles everything up.' He patted his coat pockets, felt in his vest. 'Run in and get me a couple cigars.'

waistcoat

Bruce hesitated, his eyes on Enich. 'Run!' his father said harshly.

Reluctantly he released the colt's halter rope and started for the house. At the door he looked back, and his father and Enich were talking together, so low that their words didn't carry to where he stood. He saw his father shake his head, and Enich bend to pluck a grass stem. They were both against him; they were both sure Socks would never get well. Well, he would! There was some way.

He found the cigars, came out, watched them both light up. Disappointment was a sickness in him, and mixed with the disappointment was a question. When he could stand their silence no more, he burst out with it. 'But what are we going to do? He's got to have some place to stay.'

trestle

'Look, kiddo.' His father sat down on a sawhorse and took him by the arm. His face was serious and his voice gentle. 'We can't take him out there. He isn't well enough to walk, and we can't haul him. So Jim here has offered to buy him. He'll give you three dollars for him, and when you come back, if you want, you might be able to buy him back. That is, if he's well. It'll be better to leave him with Jim.'

'Well . . .' Bruce studied the mole on Enich's cheek. 'Can you get him better by fall, Mr Enich?'

'I wouldn't expect it,' Enich said. 'He ain't got much of a show.'

'If anybody can get him better, Jim can,' his father said. 'How's that deal sound to you?'

'Maybe when I come back he'll be all off his braces and running around like a house afire,' Bruce said. 'Maybe next time I see him I can ride him.' The mole disappeared as Enich tongued his cigar.

'Well, all right then,' Bruce said, bothered by their stony-eyed silence. 'But I sure hate to leave you behind, Socks, old boy.'

'It's the best way all around,' his father said. He talked fast, as if he were in a hurry. 'Can you take him along now?'

'Oh, gee!' Bruce said. 'Today?'

'Come on,' his father said. 'Let's get it over with.'

Bruce stood by while they trussed the colt and hoisted him into the wagon box, and when Jim climbed in he cried out, 'Hey, we forgot to put his hobbles back on.' Jim and his father looked at each other. His father shrugged. 'All right,' he said, and started putting the braces back on the trussed front legs. 'He might hurt himself if they weren't on,' Bruce said. He leaned over the endgate, stroking the white blazed face, and as the wagon pulled away he stood with tears in his eyes and the three dollars in his hand, watching the terrified straining of the colt's neck, the bony head raised above the endgate and one white eye rolling.

Five days later, in the sun-slanting, dew-wet spring morning, they stood for the last time that summer on the front porch, the loaded wagon against the front fence. The father tossed the key in his hand and kicked the doorjamb. 'Well, good-bye, Old Paint,' he said. 'See you in the fall.'

As they went to the wagon Bruce sang loudly,

Good-bye, Old Paint, I'm leavin' Cheyenne,
I'm leavin' Cheyenne, I'm goin' to Montana,
Good-bye, Old Paint, I'm leavin' Cheyenne.

'Turn it off,' his father said. 'You want to wake up the whole town?' He boosted Bruce into the back end, where he squirmed and wiggled his way neck-deep into the luggage. His mother, turning to see how he was settled, laughed at him. 'You look like a baby owl in a nest,' she said.

His father turned and winked at him. 'Open your mouth and I'll drop in a mouse.'

It was good to be leaving; the thought of the homestead was exciting. If he could have taken Socks along it would have been perfect, but he had to admit, looking around at the jammed wagon box, that there sure wasn't any room for him. He continued to sing softly as they rocked out into the road and turned east towards MacKenna's house, where they were leaving the keys.

marsh   At the low, slough-like spot that had become the town's dump ground the road split, leaving the dump like an island in the middle. The boy sniffed at the old familiar smells of rust and tar paper and ashes and refuse. He had collected a lot of old iron and tea lead and bottles and broken machinery and clocks, and once a perfectly good amber-headed cane, in that old dump ground. His father turned up the right fork, and as they passed the central part of the dump the wind, coming in from the northeast, brought a rotten, unbearable stench across them.

'Pee-you!' his mother said, and held her nose. Bruce echoed her. 'Pee-you! Pee-you-willy!' He clamped his nose shut and pretended to fall dead.

'Guess I better get to windward of that coming back,' said his father.

They woke MacKenna up and left the key and started back. The things they passed were sharp and clear to the boy. He was seeing them for the last time all summer. He noticed things he had never noticed so clearly before: how the hills came down into the river from the north like three folds in a blanket, how the stovepipe on the Chinaman's shack east of town had a little conical hat on it. He chanted at the things he saw. 'Good-bye, old Chinaman. Good-bye, old Frenchman River. Good-bye, old Dump-ground, good-bye.'

'Hold your noses,' his father said. He eased the wagon into the other fork around the dump. 'Somebody sure dumped something rotten.'

He stared ahead, bending a little, and Bruce heard him swear. He slapped the reins on the team till they trotted. 'What?' the mother said. Bruce, half rising to see what caused the speed, saw her lips go flat over her teeth, and a look on her face like the woman he had seen in the travelling dentist's chair, when the dentist dug a living nerve out of her tooth and then got down on his knees to hunt for it, and she sat there half-raised in her seat, her face lifted.

'For gosh sakes,' he said. And then he saw.

He screamed at them. 'Ma, it's Socks! Stop, Pa! It's Socks!'

His father drove grimly ahead, not turning, not speaking, and his mother shook her head without looking around. He screamed again, but neither of them turned. And when he dug down into the load, burrowing in and shaking with long smothered sobs, they still said nothing.

So they left town, and as they wound up the dugway to the south bench there was not a word among them except his father's low, 'For Christ sakes, I thought he was going to take it out of town.' None of them looked back at the view they had always admired, the flat river bottom green with spring, its village snuggled in the loops of river. Bruce's eyes, pressed against the coats and blankets under him until his sight was a red haze, could still see through it the bloated, skinned body of the colt, the chestnut hair left a little way above the hooves, the iron braces still on the broken front legs.

WALLACE STEGNER

Summat Queer on Batch

moorland

There were a old widow body 'oo 'ad a little cottage up to Batch, and 'er come to market with 'er bits to sell, and she wouldn't go 'ome no how. Well, they axed 'en, and all she'd say was, 'There's Summat Queer on Batch!' and not a word more. Well, Job Ash, 'e say to 'er, 'Never 'ee mind, my dear, I'll go up Batch for 'ee. No fear.' And 'e up and went.

silently

'Twere a bit of a unket wind up to Batch, road was lonely, and wind did blow whist. 'E got to cottage, 'twere a little cottage like, with a front door and back door opposite each other, and kitchen were one side o' passage, sitting-room were t'other side o' passage, and stairs was in cupboard. In 'e goes, front door were wide open, and 'e swing the bar acrost, and 'e go to back door, and 'e swing the bar acrost there. Then 'e take a look-see to sitting-room. Weren't no one there. Then 'e gave a look-see to kitchen. No one there neither. Then 'e rub 'is 'ands together, and 'e think o' the drubbing they lads was going to 'ave.

'E opens door – cupboard door – upstairs to bedroom. When 'e got up to bedroom, wasn't no one there neither. 'Where be they tew?' said Job and 'e come down, and front door were open – back door were open tew. Bar were set back. Well, Job 'e took a quick look-see outside back door, and it slammed tew be'ind 'im, and bar slid acrost. Well, Job, 'e took off round corner o' that 'ouse; 'e didn't stop to look – gets round by front door, as fast as 'e could, and just as 'e got to front door, that slam in 'is face tew, and bar come down acrost. Well, Job, 'e took a deep breath, 'e did, and then 'e takes a look over 'is shoulder, and there were Summat Queer standing right be'ind 'im. At that Job 'e took off down that road, like 'e were to Shepton Mallet races. 'E were a girt vleshly veller, and when 'e'd got about a mile or so, 'e sat down on a 'eap o' stoneses, and 'e puff like a pair o' bellowses, and 'e got out 'is neck-'ankercher, and 'e rub 'is face, thankful. And then 'e look down, and there's a girt vlat voot aside o' 'isn. Then 'e look up a little vurther, and there's a girt 'airy 'and by 'is knee. And then 'e look up a little bit vurther still, and there's a girt wide grin.

'That were a good race, weren't it?' sez it.

'Ar!' sez Job, 'And when I've got my breath back, us'll 'ave another!'

TRADITIONAL

Sport: the Kill

With a wild rush of scraping feet, the rabbit darted in under the flat rock. His right hind leg spat up a sliver of stone from the crag and disappeared, just as the dog's snout landed with a thud at the hole. The dog yelped as he tumbled head over heels with the force of his mad rush. The rabbit crawled along the straight groove in the crag under the rock. His claws made a rasping sound as, one after the other, his legs thrust his body forward. He left a trail of brown fur behind him. Midway he halted, panting. He saw the dog's black nose twitching and snorting at the far end of the groove in front. He painfully drew up his legs under his belly, twisted around his

head so that he could see both entrances to the groove and waited. His sides pressed against the rock as they heaved.

A boy came bounding along from the left, skipping over the boulders that lined the cliff top. In his right hand he carried a dried long willow rod. He halted on a boulder and looked about him. The dog raised his head, looked at the boy, wagged his tail and barked. The boy whooped and rushed along the crag to the rock. The dog growled joyously and, throwing back his head, he scraped madly at the hole, clawing the limestone crag impotently. The boy threw himself flat at the other end where the rabbit had entered, shut one eye and looked in. When his eye pierced the gloom and he saw the rabbit, he too growled.

The rabbit, seeing enemies on both sides, tried to stick his head through a tiny crevice to his left, where the rock rested on two cone-shaped spurs of the crag. His head entered as far as the ears and could go no farther. He lay still, one ear bent double, the other ear flat on his back, the tip quivering, fanned by the dog's breath, that came through the damp groove in a pale blue column. Then a scratching sound reached him, coming towards his hind-quarters. The boy lying on his side was pushing the dried willow rod along the groove.

The end of the rod touched the rabbit's left haunch gently. It slipped up over the haunch and tipped the rock. Then it twisted with a grating sound and got stuck in the soft fur to the left of the tail. It twisted again. The skin on the rabbit's haunches went taut as it gathered around the tip of the rod. The rabbit started, held his breath and pulled his head suddenly from the crevice. He was stretching back his right leg to crawl away from the rod when he saw the dog's red tongue lolling between white fangs at the far end in front of him. With his right hind leg crooked at the thigh, he paused, his eyes blinking, his whiskers twitching, his ears pressed down into his contracted neck. Again the rod grated and twisted. The skin of his stomach was drawn up to the ball of skin and fur that was gathering around the tip of the rod. Again the rod twisted. The skin around his crutch went taut.

The boy cursed. A spur of the crag had bruised his hip. He grunted and said 'Hs-s-s-s' fiercely. The dog thrust his muzzle abruptly at the hole and barked. The bark re-echoed through the groove and the fur on the rabbit's neck quivered. The rabbit closed his eyes and bent down his head. The strong smell of the dog's breath was stifling him. Then the boy drew in a deep breath and tried to twist the rod again. His sweating hands slipped on the dried willow. The rod was too taut to turn. All the skin on the rabbit's body was as taut as the skin of a drum. The claws of his right hind leg gripped the crag with such force that their points were blunted. The dog raised his head and walked back a few paces to smell a snail that was crawling along the crag. Then he came back to the hole again, raised his left fore paw and cocked his head sideways.

Slowly, carefully, the boy began to pull the rod. For a few moments the pressure was so gradual that the rabbit did not feel himself being pulled. Then suddenly his right hind leg that was bearing the weight of his body slipped backwards with a scraping sound that ended in a thud. His whole body began to slip, bumping against the crag, the fore feet pawing the ground. He allowed himself to slip back gradually, too dazed to resist. The dog sniffed cautiously at his hole. Then fiercely. He thought the rabbit was escaping. Darting across the rock to the boy, he yelped and thrust his snout down between the boy's face and the hole. Then he whined and darted back again to his own hole.

The rabbit was within a foot of the boy's hand at the mouth of the hole when the rod caught in a cleft, where the rock rested on a spur of the crag just within the mouth of the groove. The boy cursed and gave the rod a jerk. It failed to move. Then he pushed it back. The rabbit drew up his hind legs under him feeling the tension relaxed. Then the boy tried to give the rod another twist to free it. He had twisted it around slightly when the skin on the rabbit's haunch burst with a snap. The rabbit jerked his head up and down suddenly and, striking the crag with his four feet, thrust himself forward with a wild squeal. The dog thrust his body at his hole furiously, cutting his muzzle against the crag. Then he lay on his belly, his eyes watery, his jaws slightly open. The boy jumped to his knees and, seizing the rod with both hands, he wrenched it clean out of the groove with a large patch of the rabbit's skin at its tip. The rabbit blinded by the pain crawled straight ahead heedless of the dog. The dog drew back his snout. His tail stretched out. His eyes half closed. His chest shivered. The rabbit's head appeared. There was a smothered squeal and then a low crack as the dog's fangs met through the rabbit's neck.

The dog tossed the rabbit in triumph over his head as the boy leaped across the rock. The boy grabbed the rabbit's hind legs and kicked the dog fiercely on the ribs. The dog dropped the rabbit and ran back whining. The boy held up the body heaving as if it were leaping fences in its death agony. 'High' he hissed through his teeth.

Then he bashed the rabbit's head on the rock.

LIAM O'FLAHERTY

Spoil the Child

The first morning pa was gone, I tried to ride one of the mules. I didn't think that would hurt, because the mules were unharnessed anyway. But Maude told ma, and ma licked me. Ma was in the wagon, and she wouldn't have seen. I told Maude I'd remember.

Pa left about six in the morning while ma still slept. 'Goin' after meat?' I asked him. He had his rifle.

He nodded.

'Kin I go?'

'Stay with ma, sonny,' he said. 'She ain't well.'

'You said I could hunt –'

'You stay with ma, sonny.'

Maude got up a few minutes after that. I could see pa like a black dot out on the prairie. I pointed to him.

I said: 'That's pa out there huntin'.'

Maude was combing her hair, not paying a lot of attention to me. Then I tried to ride the mule. Pa would never let me ride his horse. It was only half-broken, cost four hundred dollars. Ma was always saying we could have lived a year on what that horse cost.

Maude woke ma. My mother was a tall, thin woman, tired looking. She wasn't well. I could see that she wasn't well.

'Dave, get off that mule,' she said. 'Where's pa?'

'Went out to hunt.'

'Come here. Can't ever get it into your head to behave.' I went over, and she slapped my face. 'Don't bother them mules. When'll he be back? We can't stay here.'

'He didn't say.'

dried buffalo
droppings

'Get some chips for a fire,' ma told me. 'My land, I never seen such a lazy, shiftless boy.' But she didn't say it the way she always did, as if she would want to bite my head off. She seemed too tired to really care.

I guess ma licked me every day. She said I was bad – a lot worse than you'd expect from a boy of twelve. You didn't expect them to be bad that young.

'You learn to leave the mules alone,' Maude called.

'You shut up,' I told her. Maude was fifteen, and pretty. She had light hair, and a thin, delicate face. Ma said that someday Maude would be a lady. She didn't expect much from me. She said I would be like pa.

I walked away from the wagon, looking for chips. By now, pa was out of sight, and where he had gone the prairie was just a roll of yellow and brown, a thread of cloud above it. It frightened me to be alone on the prairie. Pa laughed at it, and called it a big meadow. But it frightened me.

We had been on the prairie for a week now. Pa said in another few weeks we'd reach Fort Lee, due west. He said that if he had cattle stock, he'd settle down right on the prairie. This way, he'd cross the mountains, grow fruit, maybe, in California. Ma never believed much he said.

I went back to the wagon and started a fire. Ma had gone inside, and Maude sat on the driver's seat.

'You might gimme a hand,' I told Maude.

'I don't see you overworking,' Maude said.

'You'd better learn to shut up.'

From inside the wagon, ma yelled: 'You hold your tongue, Dave, or I'll wallop you!'

'You're a little beast,' Maude said.

'You wait,' I told her.

I went to the keg, drew some water, and set it up to boil. I could tell by the sound that there wasn't a lot of water left in the keg. Pa had said we'd reach water soon.

When I came back to the fire, I glanced up at the sky. It was an immense bowl of hot blue, bare except for a single buzzard that turned slowly, like a fish swimming. I guess I forgot. I kept looking up at the buzzard.

Ma climbed down from the wagon slowly. 'You're the same as your pa,' she said. 'Lazy an' bad.' Her face was tight-drawn. For the past few weeks she had hardly smiled, and now it seemed that she wouldn't smile again.

'And fresh,' Maude said.

I put the water on the fire, not saying anything.

'Spare the rod and spoil the child,' ma said.

Then her face twisted in pain, and she leaned against the wagon. 'Well, don't stand there,' she told me. 'Water the mules.'

I went to the keg. I knew there wasn't enough water for the mules. I hoped Pa would come back soon; I had a funny, awful fear of what would happen if he didn't come back soon. I kept glancing out at the prairie.

Pa had an itch in his feet. Ma said I would grow up the same way – having an itch in my feet. She was always sorry that she had married a man with an itch in his feet. Sometimes she said that the war had done it, that after the war between the North and the South, men were either broken or had to keep moving, like pa. Always west.

We lived in Columbus. Then we moved to St Louis; then to

D

Topeka. Pa couldn't stop, and ma got more and more worn out. She said that a wild land was no place to raise children. It was hard on ma, all right. Pa didn't do much, except when we were moving west, and then he would be like a different person. Ma never complained to him. She licked me instead.

I gave the mules enough water to cover the bottoms of their pails.

Ma came over, said: 'That's not enough water.'

'There ain't a damn sight more.'

'Don't swear!' ma exclaimed. She clapped a hand across my head.

'He's always swearing,' Maude said. 'Thinks he's grown up.'

Ma stared at me a moment, dully; then she went over and prepared breakfast. It was gruel and hardtack.

hard biscuit

'Fresh meat would be good,' ma said. She looked over the prairie, maybe looking for pa. I knew how much she cared for pa. She would talk a lot about itching feet, but that didn't matter.

After breakfast, I gave the mules some oats, and Maude cleaned up the dishes. I kept glancing at Maude, and she knew what I meant. She didn't care, until ma went back into the wagon. It hurt me to look at ma.

'He'll be back soon, I guess,' ma said. Then she climbed into the wagon. It was a big sixteen-foot wagon, the kind they called freighters, with a hooped top, covered over with dirty brown canvas.

Maude said: 'You leave me alone.'

'I'll leave you alone now,' I told Maude. 'I gotta leave you alone now. Maybe you know what's the matter with ma?'

'That's none of your business,' Maude said.

'It's my business, all right.'

'You're just a kid.'

I went to the back of the wagon and pulled out pa's carbine. It was the one he had used during the war, a short cavalry gun.

Ma saw me; she lay inside, and I could hear her breathing hard. She said: 'What're you up to now; pa back?'

'Not yet.'

'Well, you tell me soon as he gets back. And don't get into any mischief.'

'All right.'

In front of the wagon, I sat down on a feed box, and cleaned the gun with an old rag. Maude watched me. Finally, she said: 'I'm gonna tell ma you're fooling with pa's gun.'

'You keep your mouth shut.'

Ma groaned softly then, and we both turned around and looked at the wagon. I felt little shivers crawl up and down my spine. Where was pa? He should have been back already. I put down the gun and walked around the wagon. In a circle, the prairie rose and fell, like a sea of whispering yellow grass. There was nothing there, no living thing.

Maude was crying. 'Why don't pa come back?' she said.

I didn't answer her. I guess it occurred to me for the first time that pa might not come back. I felt like crying. I felt like getting into a corner and crying. I hadn't felt so small for a long time. It would be a comfort to have ma lick me now. You get licked, and you know you're a kid, and you don't have to worry about anything else.

I said to Maude: 'Go inside the wagon and stay with ma.'

'Don't you order me around.'

'All right,' I said. I turned my back on her. I didn't hold much with girls when they're that age.

Then Maude went inside the wagon. I heard her crying, and I heard ma say: 'You stop that crying right now.'

I loaded the carbine. I untethered one of the mules, climbed onto it, and set out across the prairie in the direction pa had taken. I didn't know just what I'd do, but I knew it was time pa came back.

It wasn't easy, riding the mule just with harness straps. Mules have a funny gait. And we didn't go very fast. I was glad ma and Maude were in the wagon, otherwise ma would probably lick the pants off me.

In about a half hour, the wagon was just a tiny black dot. It might have been anything. I kept glancing at the sun to remember the direction I had taken. Then a swell hid the wagon. I kept on going. I knew that if I stopped, even for a little while, I'd cry my head off.

I saw a coyote. He stood like a dog and watched me. An antelope hopped close, and I might have shot at them. But I couldn't bring myself to fire a rifle there. It would have done something to me.

I found pa. I guess I had been riding for about an hour when I saw him, over to one side. A buzzard flapped up, and I felt my throat tighten until I thought it would choke me. I didn't want to go over to him. I got down from the mule, and I walked over slowly. But I didn't want to; something made me.

He was dead, all right. Maybe it was Indians and maybe it wasn't; I didn't know. He was shot four times, and his gun was gone.

The buzzard wouldn't go away; I shot the buzzard. I didn't cry. The carbine kicked back and made my shoulder ache. I was thinking about how pa always called me an undersized, freckled little runt. He said I wouldn't grow up. Maybe that's why I didn't cry.

I went away a little distance and sat down. I didn't look at pa. I tried to remember where we were, what pa had told me about going west. When I thought of ma, I had a sense of awful fear. Suppose it happened now.

The mule walked over and nuzzled my shoulder. I was glad the mule was there then. If he wasn't, I don't know what I would have done.

Pa had to be buried. I knew that men had to be buried, but I couldn't do it. The prairie was hard, baked mud. I went back to pa and stood over him; I guess that was the hardest thing I had ever done in my life. I straightened his clothes. I pulled off his boots. Men in the West were always talking about dying with their boots on. I didn't know how it meant anything, one way or another, but I thought pa would be pleased if he didn't have his boots on.

Then I climbed up on the mule and started back for the wagon. I tried not to think that I was twelve years old. If you get to thinking about that, then you're no good at all. When I got back, ma would lick me plenty.

The mule must have found its way back, because I didn't pay much attention to that. I let the reins loose, holding onto the harness straps, and I kept swallowing. Then I saw the wagon.

I thought: 'I can't tell ma now – maybe later.' Nobody had ever told me about a thing like that, but I knew it wouldn't do to tell ma now. I guess I only felt it instinctively, but I knew that the importance wasn't in pa any more. All that was important was life, and life was just a fleck of dust in the prairie. It was like a nightmare to think of the distance of the prairie, and how we were alone.

I rode up to the wagon, and Maude and ma were both standing next to it. I could tell from ma's face how worried she had been about me.

'There he is!' Maude screamed.

Ma said: 'I guess there ain't nothing a body can do with you, Dave. Get off that mule.'

I slipped off, tethered the mule. My whole body was twisted up with the strain of keeping what I had seen off my face. I came over to ma.

'Where have you been?' she demanded.

'Hunting.'

'I reckon there's nothing else for a little loafer like you. Spare the rod and spoil the child. Come here.'

I went over and bent down, and she walloped me a bit, not too hard. She wasn't very strong then, I guess. I cried, but I wasn't crying because of the licking. I had had worse lickings than that and never opened my mouth. But it seemed to break the tension inside of me, and I had to cry. I went over and sat down with my back against one of the wagon wheels.

Maude walked past me and said: 'I guess that learned you.'

I just looked at her, without answering. I took out my jack-knife and began to pare at one of the wagon boards. Then my eyes travelled to the water keg.

I got up and went around to ma. She was still standing there, staring off across the prairie in the direction pa had gone.

Without turning, she said to me: 'Seen anything of your pa?'

'No.'

The sun was westward now, a splotch of red that blazed the whole prairie into a fire. I could get a little of how ma felt; I could see the loneliness.

'Get a fire going,' she said. 'He ought to have enough sense to come back early. Stop that whimpering. God help a woman when a man has itching feet.'

I gathered chips and started the fire. When I took water from the keg for mush, the keg was just about empty. I didn't mention that to ma. She went about preparing supper slowly, awkwardly, and Maude watched her, frightened.

Ma kept glancing at the west.

'Be dark soon,' I said.

'Guess pa'll be here any minute,' ma said dully. I could tell that she didn't believe that.

'I guess so,' I nodded.

We ate without speaking much. Ma didn't eat a great deal. As soon as we had finished, she went into the wagon.

Maude was saying: 'I don't see how I can clean dishes without water. You fetch some water, Dave.'

'There ain't no water,' I said.

Maude stared at me, her eyes wide and frightened. She had heard stories, just the same as I had, about pilgrims who ran out of water. She opened her mouth to say something.

'What about ma?' I asked her quietly, nodding at the wagon.

'Why don't pa come back?'

'Ain't no sense thinking about pa if he ain't here. What about ma? I guess it won't be long.'

She shook her head.

'You don't need to be scared,' I muttered. 'It won't do no good to be scared. I reckon the worst part of this trip is over.'

'Where's pa?' she whispered. 'What happened?'

'How do I know what happened? You girls make me sick. I never seen anything to beat you girls.'

I got up and went over to the water keg. I shook it, hoping, without having any reason to hope. I knew it was just about empty. We had plenty of food – dried meat and meal and dried beans – enough to last a month, I guess. But ma would need water.

Maude was crying.

'Why don't you go to bed?' I told her.

'Don't order me around.'

'Well, you go to bed,' I said. 'Go in and sleep with ma. I'll stay out here.'

'You're not big enough to stay out here alone,' Maude said, but I knew she was afraid to stay inside the wagon with ma. I knew how she felt, and I didn't blame her for the way she felt, she was such a kid, with ma petting her all the time. We couldn't talk it over between ourselves, and that would have made it a lot better. But we couldn't.

'I'm plenty big enough,' I said.

Inside the wagon ma groaned, and out on the prairie a coyote was barking. There's nothing like a coyote barking to make your insides crawl. I was all shivers, and I could see that Maude wanted to stay close to me. But that wouldn't have made it any better.

'Get in the wagon, damn you!' I cried. I was glad ma couldn't hear me swear. Ma would lick me good and plenty when I swore like that.

Surprised, Maude stared at me. Then, without a word, she went into the wagon.

I stood there, outside, for a while. It had grown quite dark. In the sky there was a faint, reflected light of the sun, but it was quite dark. I walked over to the wagon and picked up one of the mule blankets that hung on the shafts. It was a warm night, summertime; I decided to put the blanket under the wagon and lie down on it.

I heard Maude saying her prayers in the wagon, but no sound from ma. I couldn't say my prayers. Usually, ma saw to it that I did, but tonight I couldn't say a word aloud. I tried, opening my mouth, but no words came out. I thought them, as much as I could. I tried not to think about pa. Spreading the blanket, I lay down on it, holding the carbine close to me. It seemed a part of pa and all that was left; I hugged it.

I couldn't sleep. I tried for a long time, but I couldn't sleep. It was quite dark now, with no moon in the sky. The mules were moving restlessly; probably because they wanted water.

I think I dozed a little. When I opened my eyes again, the moon was just coming up, yellow and bloated. I felt chilled thoroughly.

Bit by bit, what had happened during the day came back, and now it was all more real than it had been in the daytime. While I lay there, thinking about it, I heard horses' hoofs; at first not noticing them, and only becoming aware of them when the horses bulked out of the the night, two men riding slowly.

They were in the moonlight, and I was hidden in the shadow of the wagon. They didn't see me. They stopped just about a dozen yards from the wagon, sitting on their horses and eyeing the mules. The mules moved restlessly.

When I realized they were Indians I couldn't move, just lay there and watched them. They were naked to the waist, with their hair in two stiff braids to their shoulders. They both carried rifles.

I thought of pa. I thought of screaming to wake Maude and ma. I thought: 'If they shot pa –'

They were cutting loose the mules.

I felt for the carbine, twisted around, so I lay on my belly. One of the men had dismounted and was coming towards the wagon. He held his gun in one hand and had drawn a knife with the other. I sighted the centre of his breast and fired.

I remember how the sound blasted out the silence of the prairie. In the wagon, someone screamed. The Indian stopped, seemed to stare at me, swayed a bit, and crumpled to the ground. I remember the sharp pain in my shoulder from the blow of the recoil.

The mounted man's horse had wheeled about. He pulled it back, and fired at me. The shot threw sand in my face. I had a few cartridges and caps in my pocket, and I tried frantically to reload. The cartridges slipped through my fingers.

Then the Indian was gone. He had taken the other horse with him, and I heard their hoofs thundering across the prairie. I dropped the carbine. My shoulder ached terribly. Inside the wagon, Maude was whimpering, my mother groaning.

I climbed from under the wagon. The Indian lay on his back, his face hard and twisted. I stood there, looking at him.

Maude climbed down out of the wagon. 'What is it?' she cried. Then she saw the Indian and screamed.

'All right – I shot him.'

She stood there, holding her hand to her mouth.

'You get back in the wagon. I guess he killed pa, all right. Don't tell that to ma.'

She shook her head. Ma was groaning. 'I can't go back,' Maude said.

'Why?'

And then I knew. I should have known from the way ma was

groaning. I went up to Maude and slapped her face. She didn't seem to feel it. I slapped her again.

'Get in there with ma.'

'I can't – it's dark.'

'Get in there!' I yelled.

We had lanterns on the outside of the wagon. I took one and lit it. I wasn't trembling so much now. I gave the lantern to Maude, who was still standing the way she had been before.

'Go inside,' I said.

Maude climbed into the wagon, taking the lantern with her. Then I cried. I crouched under the wagon, clutching the carbine and crying.

Finally, I went over to the Indian. I forced myself to do that. He lay half across the rifle he had carried. I pulled it out, and it was my father's rifle, all right.

I don't know how long I stood there holding the rifle. Then I put it under the seat, along with the carbine. I didn't want to look at the wagon.

I walked over to the mules, led them over to the shafts. It was hard to harness them. I had to balance myself on the shafts to get at their backs. When it was done, I ached all over, and my shoulder was swollen where the carbine had rested.

I climbed to the driver's seat. The curtains were down, and I couldn't see into the wagon, but the light still burned. Taking down pa's whip, I let it go onto the mules' backs. I had seen pa do that, and sometimes he let me try. The whip was fourteen feet long and I couldn't do much with it, but I got the mules moving. They had to keep moving. We had to find water.

At night, under the moon, the prairie was black and silver at the same time. Somehow, it didn't frighten me, the way it had during the day. I sat there thinking, I guess, of nothing at all, only awfully aware of the change inside me.

We drove on like that. I kept the mules at a slow pace, so the freighter wouldn't roll much. I was very tired, and after a while I didn't use the whip at all.

Then Maude came out of the wagon, sat down next to me. She looked at me and I looked at her, but she didn't say anything. She pressed close to me.

I whistled at the mules.

Inside the wagon something was whimpering. It made me tremble to hear that.

'Reckon we'll find water soon,' I told Maude.

She nodded mechanically. Her head kept nodding and I dozed,

myself. I guess I kept dozing through the night, fell asleep towards morning.

Maude woke me. The wagon had stopped, and the sun was an hour up. The mules had stopped on the bank of a slow, brown stream, lined with cottonwoods as far as I could see.

Maude was pointing at the water.

'Don't you start crying now,' I said, rubbing my eyes.

'I won't,' Maude nodded.

Ma called me, not very loud: 'Dave come here.'

I climbed inside the wagon. Ma was lying on the bed, her arm curled around something. I peered at it.

'Do you know?' she said.

'I reckon I do. I reckon it's a boy. Girls ain't much use.'

Ma was crying – not much; her eyes were just wetting themselves slowly.

'Where are we?' ma asked me.

'We been travelling through the night. There's a river out there. I guess we don't need to worry about water.'

'All night – pa back?'

I said, slowly: 'I killed an Indian last night, ma. He had pa's gun.'

Then she just stared at me, and I stood there, shifting from one foot to another, wanting to run away. But I stood there. It must have been about five minutes, and she didn't say anything at all. The baby was whimpering.

Then she said: 'You harnessed the mules?'

'Uh-huh. Maude didn't help me –'

Ma said: 'You don't tease Maude. You don't tease Maude, or I'll take a stick to you. I never seen a boy like you for teasing.'

'Uh-huh,' I nodded.

'Just like your pa,' ma whispered. 'It don't pay to have a man whose heels are always itching – it don't pay.'

'No use cryin',' I said.

Ma said: 'What are we going to do?'

'Go on west. Ain't hard now to go a few hundred miles more. Reckon it won't be hard. Pa said –'

Ma was staring at me, her mouth trembling. I hadn't ever seen her look just like that before. I wanted to put my head down on her breast, hide it there.

I couldn't do that. I said: 'Pa told me. We'll go west.'

Then I went outside. I sat down on the wagon seat, looking at the river. I heard the baby making noises.

I said to Maude: 'A man feels funny – with a kid.'

HOWARD FAST

The Dog with a Million Fleas

I heard my mother calling me and groaned, time to get up again. The edges of my window panes sparkled with frost and the sky looked grey, as though it were going to snow. And then I remembered, it was Saturday, the best day of the whole week. I lay there warm and snug and planned what I would do. I know! I would go to the copse. As long as I can remember my sister and I have made up special names for people, places and things. 'The Grand Canyon' for instance is a dale we often visit for picnics and 'Little Egypt' is a hillock with some trees on top, and The Copse is a name which we gave to the grounds surrounding an old house which has since been pulled down. It is a magic sort of place where one can always find something unusual, there my sister and I have spent many a happy hour wandering about and imagining all sorts of things there. We have often seen a family of hedgehogs, and are careful not to frighten them as they are rather timid at first. It is a favourite haunt of birds, and there is an old square well, but we pretend it is a wishing well, and we have found two beehives tucked away among the undergrowth, empty now but once they were used. The house was standing then and people lived in it and I expect they were very happy at least my sister and I like to think so, and so I decided to go to the copse again, and I wondered what I would discover today. The best things always happen to me on a Saturday except Christmas and birthdays as they happen on any day of the week.

I dressed and had my breakfast, mummy made me put on two pairs of socks and then my wellingtons as she said it was going to snow. I put my scarf and gloves on too and pretended I was an explorer in the arctic wastes. I slipped my penknife into my pocket and two russets from the box in the pantry. In the autumn when our apples are ready for picking, we gather them and wrap them up in paper, then in winter we have a good supply to munch at, they have a nice taste and the skins are very wrinkled, at night mummy puts a bowl on the hearth and we all help ourselves.

Now my penknife is a very special one, and I have never seen another like it, and I feel very proud when people ask to see it, for it has two blades, a corkscrew, a saw, a tin opener, a screwdriver, an pointed blade awl and even a pair of scissors. My uncle gave it to me for my birthday four years ago, it was not new when he gave it to me, for he had it during the war, and he knew that I admired it more than anything else in the world, and although I have had lots of nice presents for Christmas and birthdays this one seemed my best.

So I felt very happy as I went down the lane with the penknife and apples in my pocket. I wished I had brought my dog Dandy with me as he loves exploring too, he is not an ordinary dog, everyone else seems to have dogs like poodles, dachshunds and dogs like that, but my dog is a cross-bred terrier, some people say he's only a mongrel, and I tell them that he's cleverer than any dog I've ever met, he can play hide and seek and he doesn't cheat either! You can leave him

in the potting shed, and tell him to stay and hide his eyes, then hide yourself and whistle him, and he always finds you, he joins in all our games and he is four years old, and we bought him for twelve and six from the Manchester Dogs Home and mummy says he's the best twelve and six-pennyworth she has ever seen. Any way I must tell you about my visit to the copse when I got there the ground was white with frost and it made everything look different. I didn't see any birds or anything at all, the copse seemed quiet and deserted but a little dog with a rough curly coat came trotting up to me, it barked at first but when I talked to it a little it wagged its tail and let me pat it, every so often it shook itself sat down and started to scratch furiously and then I heard a whistle and looked up and saw a boy, he was about 9 years old and had a nice friendly sort of face and he smiled at me. 'That's my dog,' he said, 'He's called Ruff.' I told him I had a dog too. All the time we were talking I was looking at him. He looked very cold as his clothes seemed too small for him, his jacket sleeves were very short and his thin wrists stuck out, and his hands were very red, he kept rubbing them together. He was a thin sort of boy and very cheerful and I liked him a lot. He said he had never been to the copse before. I showed him my pen-knife while we were talking and I could see he thought it was marvellous. He kept on opening and shutting the blades and cutting little bits of wood that lay about. And then he said rather sadly, 'I wish I had one like it,' and I said, 'Why don't you ask your father to buy you one for Christmas?' He said very quickly, 'I haven't got a father.' I could tell by the way he spoke he didn't want to say any more, so I offered him an apple. He bit a piece off for his dog and then asked me what made the skins wrinkled like that. 'It's a russet,' I said. 'My father picks them from the trees and puts them by for winter.' 'Have you got your own apple trees,' he said in surprise, 'How many have you got.' I was just going to say eight when I stopped. How could I say I had eight apple trees when he hadn't even got a father. 'Oh we've only got one,' I said, 'And it's not a very good one either.' 'This tastes all right to me,' he said. All the time he had been talking to me, his little dog had been running round and jumping up at him and licking his hands, you could see the dog loved him. And he would bend down and rub the dog's ears and fuss him as if he loved him too, and every so often the dog would shake himself violently and scratch himself first one place and then another, it made me tickle all over just to look at him. 'Why does he keep shaking and scratching,' I asked. 'Oh!' he said, 'He can't help it, he's got fleas.' 'Fleas?' I said. 'Yes,' he said proudly, 'He's got about a million of them.' 'Doesn't he mind,' I said. 'Oh no,' he answered. 'He's always had them.' What with scratching and shaking and jumping and licking he was the funniest little dog I have ever seen.

The boy took something from his pocket. 'Look at this,' he said. It was a large marble and it had a lovely coloured whirly line going round inside it. He told me to look through it, and I did so, it looked beautiful and he was very pleased when I told him it was the best one I had ever seen. 'Would you like it,' he said. 'Oh no I couldn't take it,' I told him. 'Go on,' he said, 'I want you to have it.' He pressed it in my hand and said, 'I must go now. I'll come again next week.' He whistled his dog who was scratching as though his life depended on it, he bounded after the boy, and off they went, when he came to the trees he turned and waved, and I waved back, I still had the marble in one hand and my penknife in the the other, in a moment the boy and dog had gone.

I stood there feeling very miserable I had such a lot of things, I could easily have given him the knife. He only had a marble and he had given that to me.

I went home and went up to my room to think it over, my dog came with me, I sat on my bed and he pushed his nose into my hands, he knew how I felt, he may not have fleas but he's very understanding. I put the marble and penknife in my top drawer and went downstairs. I told mummy all about it and asked her what I should have done, and she asked me what I would do if the same thing should happen all over again and I said that I would give him the knife, so I made up my mind that if he came the next week I would give it him. Now in nearly all books I have read the stories have had happy endings but this one hasn't. Although I went back to the copse many times I didn't see the boy or dog again. It doesn't seem the same magic place any more, the workmen have been and cut down most of the trees and it's just a large space now.

Mummy said when I asked her why, 'Nothing ever stands still, things are changing all the time.'

It all happened a long time ago, but I still have the penknife and marble. I don't suppose I will ever see him again, it used to make me feel unhappy but when I think of the boy now I don't feel sad about him any more. My mother said that anyone with a nice little dog like Ruff couldn't help feeling happy. So I think of him as I last saw him waving to me through the trees with his little dog jumping up and down and running round him, the dog that loved him best in the world, the dog with a million fleas !

STUART ALBERT WIDDOWS *aged 12*

The Animal That Drank Up Sound

1

One day across the lake where echoes come now
an animal that needed sound came down. He gazed
enormously, and instead of making any, he took
away from, sound: the lake and all the land
went dumb. A fish that jumped went back like a knife,
and the water died. In all the wilderness around he
drained the rustle from the leaves into the mountainside
and folded a quilt over the rocks, getting ready
to store everything the place had known; he buried –
thousands of autumns deep – the noise that used to come there.

Then that animal wandered on and began to drink
the sound out of all the valleys – the croak of toads,
and all the little shiny noise grass blades make.
He drank till winter, and then looked out one night
at the stilled places guaranteed around by frozen
peaks and held in the shallow pools of starlight.
It was finally tall and still, and he stopped on the highest
ridge, just where the cold sky fell away
like a perpetual curve, and from there he walked on silently,
and began to starve.

When the moon drifted over that night the whole world lay
just like the moon, shining back that still
silver, and the moon saw its own animal dead
on the snow, its dark absorbent paws and quiet
muzzle, and thick, velvet, deep fur.

2

After the animal that drank sound died, the world
lay still and cold for months, and the moon yearned
and explored, letting its dead light float down
the west walls of canyons and then climb its delighted
soundless way up the east side. The moon
owned the earth its animal had faithfully explored.
The sun disregarded the life it used to warm.

But on the north side of a mountain, deep in some rocks.
a cricket slept. It had been hiding when that animal
passed, and as spring came again this cricket waited,
afraid to crawl out into the heavy stillness.

Think how deep the cricket felt, lost there
in such a silence – the grass, the leaves, the water,
the stilled animals all depending on such a little
thing. But softly it tried – 'Cricket!' – and back like a river
from that one act flowed the kind of world we know,
first whisperings, then moves in the grass and leaves;
the water splashed, and a big night bird screamed.

It all returned, our precious world with its life and sound,
where sometimes loud over the hill the moon,
wild again, looks for its animal to roam, still,
down out of the hills, any time.
But somewhere a cricket waits.

It listens now, and practises at night.

WILLIAM STAFFORD

The sad happy ending story of

The Bald Twit Lion

A story for very all ages

Monkey involved in Bald Twit Lion story. Also cashier at Zoo.

Once, twice and thrice upon a time there lived a Jungle. It started at the bottom and went upwards till it reached the monkeys, who had been waiting years for the trees to reach them, and as soon as they did the monkeys invented climbing down. Most trees were made of wood, and so were the rest. Trees never spoke, not even to each other, so they never said much (actually one tree did once say 'much' but nobody believed him), they never said 'fish' either, not even on Fridays. It was a really good Jungle: great scarlet lilies, yellow irises, thousands of grasses all grew very happily, and this Jungle was always on time. Some people are always late, like the late King George V. But not this Jungle.

This Jungle became very, very popular with lots of wonderful animals; there was absolutely no shortage of them and therefore the Jungle was ever so busy. This Jungle was called the Bozzollika-Dowser Jungle. Because. There was no organization there, but *every-thing* worked out perfectly. Some scientists tried to make an organ-

A Hippochondriac who was too ill to appear in the Bald Twit Lion story. So . . .

ized Jungle of plastic, but it didn't improve conditions and the scientists left saying, 'Let's go to the moon instead,' and as there is nothing on the moon it seemed the best place for them. Men kept coming to the Jungle looking for gold, diamonds, gas and oil. Whereas simple animals could live without the things, brilliant man couldn't, in fact he'd forgotten how to. One thing he never forgot was how to have wars and say, 'Oh dear, how sad,' when children were killed by bombs. The animals left these things called men alone. In return for this kindness man killed them, cut off their skins and put them on the floor; cut their heads off and stuck them on the walls. But if ever an animal killed a man, it was in *all* the newspapers.

But this story is a hap-hap-happy story, about animals. One day in the middle of the Jungle, near a village called Pongoland, a big lion called Mr Gronk had an attack of strongness. He was twenty-one that day and had been given the key to the Jungle, so he put on a fierce look and then, leaping in the air, he gave the biggest, loudest

He would have looked even sillier as a one-legged bald twit lion.

Bald Twit Lion leaping and saying, 'Tsu! Tsu!'

roar in the world. 'ROAR – ROAR R☺AR!! R☺AR!!! ' he went;
in fact he roared so loud that it loosened all the roots of his
hair and tinkle tinkle all his lovely mane fell off, and landed on the
ground PLIP-PLAP-PLOP 200,000 times, one for every hair. Suddenly Mr Gronk the lion saw himself in the Daily Mirror and, oh!
he saw that he was now bald! A *Bald* Lion? 'Oh dearie me, I'll be
the laughing stock of the hyenas,' he said. So he unroared,
' ЯАоЯ! ЯАоЯ! ЯАоЯ! ', but his hairs didn't go back in, they just
lay there smiling up at him, in hairy (that's hair language). Poor
Mr Gronk, he now looked like a bald twit lion. As a passing hippopotamus said, 'I am a passing hippopotamus,' and went on to say,
'you look like a bald hairless twit lion.' When the lion heard that, he
became naughty, angry and was just about to do a BIG roar, but
no! he stopped, *just* in time; he'd better not roar any more, or
something else might drop off him! He would look even sillier as a
one-legged bald hairless twit lion, so, from then on when he was
angry, he could only say very quietly, 'Tsu-tsu-tsu', and there is
nothing funnier than a bald hairless twit lion called Mr Gronk leaping about the Jungle going, 'Tsu-tsu-tsu'.

One night when he was having tea (Lyons) he said, 'I can't go on
being bald. It's a big problem: I must find a solution.' So he
squeezed every tube in the Jungle but not one had the right solution
in it. Then he thought, 'I'll try straining very hard and think about
growing hairs.' So he strained, *strained* and STRAINED, but it only
made his eyes water and his nose bleed. Everyone laughed. His own

flea left him. 'There's nowhere to hide on a bald twit lion,' he said and hopped  it. He bribed a part-time hairy ant-eater to sit on his head; it really looked like real hair, but the lion got hick-ups and, each time, hairy ant-eater fell off. 'I'm off,' he said (which was obvious as he'd just fallen off). Lion was heart-broken. 'Sad growls,' he said and then did what no lion had ever done before, not even in the Ark, he laid himself down on the World and cried. 'Boo-hoo, boo-hairless-hoo.' The animals, having no television, gathered around him to look and feel sad. 'He must have an upset tummy,' said a monkey's stomach. 'I would say he's had bad news,' said a teenage coconut. 'Rubbish,' said a daft penguin and his cousin. 'Lions never get bad news. No one can ever get near enough to tell them.' 'I think I know what it is,' said an owl from his bed. 'His great-great grandfather was a baboon who tried to fly to the sun, and he has just heard about it.' All the animals shook their heads, and some fell off. It wasn't a very good day for the Jungle or the animals. To make it worse a mole made a mole hill that turned into a mountain and hurt its back. By now Bald Twit Lion had cried so much he ran out of tears, and had to drink two gallons of water (one for each eye). Then off he went again. 'Boo . . . -hoo. Boo-

Daft Penguin

Daft Penguin's First Cousin

Teenaged Coca-nut

CHAPTER TWO

hoo.' All hope was not lost. A voice above him said, 'Please stop crying – I've got rheumatism and all this water doesn't help.' It was a lovely cross-eyed white crow (he had once been a black one, but he went colour blind making a rainbow). 'Things could be worse,' said Crow. 'You could be a Hamlet pencil, 2B or not 2B . . .' 'Oh, shut up,' said Lion. 'You're even making my misery miserabler.' 'Listen,' said the Crow landing on Lion's nose. 'Why don't you get all the other lions to shave their heads bald then yours wouldn't notice!' Bald Twit Lion jumped to his paws. 'Whoopee! Saved! I've been saved. Mr White Crow, thanks,' and he gave Crow a piece of knotted string as a present. Round the Jungle raced Hairless Bald Twit Lion: 'Shave all your heads, or your legs will drop off!' he shouted. Soon the Jungle was alive with the sound of frightened lions shaving their heads to stop their legs falling off. In fractions it went like this:

Shave all your heads or your legs will drop off =

$$\frac{fear}{shaving} = \text{Bald Twit Lions.}$$

Next morning the Jungle was full of hairless bald twit lions with legs and Mr Gronk was delighted.

So all that day the Jungle was a mass of leaping bald-headed lions, all looking very pleased with themselves for saving their legs. But, oh dear! Everything and every non-lion animal burst out laughing. One monkey laughed so much he fell out of his tree and krupled his blutzon, but worse still, the lady lions were all furious with fury at their silly bald husbands, so they refused to talk or growl to them. All the bald lions realized they had been spoofed. But then, along came a holy man called Daniel. He took pity on them. 'Listen,' he said. 'I was once locked in a den of lions, and none of

The crow that stood on Bald Twit Lion's nose

them bit me, and the audience asked for their money back, so it's my turn to do *you* all a good turn.' So he did twenty good turns and became giddy. Then he sat down, and started to invent lions' wigs. He did it like this. After dark, Daniel would creep up to sleeping gorillas and snip-snip all the hairs off their chests. Daniel then stuck the hairs on a piece of rag, and glued them to the lion's head with nails, all except – Guess Who? Yes, poor old Mr Gronk the hairless bald twit lion. Because he was responsible for all the baldness, he was left out.

He became so sad he cried for forty days and forty nights and suffered from lakes on the knees. To make it worse there were ducks on the lake, they made such a noise at night he couldn't get to sleep so he got to wake. The quacking drove his knees deaf, in fact even if you hit stones at them they could not hear – they were stone deaf – and poor Mr Gronk had to tie ear trumpets to his legs so his knees could hear stones coming. What a picture of twit misery.

Now, you can't stop a story and leave Mr Gronk like that! No! He was still bald and it was this that changed his life. One day a

Daniel, snipping hairs of gorilla's chest to make lion wigs

party of tourists surprised Bald Twit, who was sleeping under a porridge tree for breakfast. The tourists couldn't believe their eyes, some couldn't even believe their teeth.

A bald lion? This must be the rarest animal in the world! Never in the history of the world had there ever been such a hanimule. It did not take long before great safaris of tourists were crowding the Jungle with cameras and flashlights. Mr Gronk's head became the most photographed bald head in the world, some people even took tape recordings of his baldness. His head got into the Top Ten Baldies; he out-balded Yul Brynner and Bing Crosby. Record companies even made long playing records of his bald head.

Happy Tail →

Sad

Poor Bald Twit Lion with deaf knees

For a time he was very happy but – whereas everyone was mad to see his bald head, no one ever came to see *him*. This was the bitter end. But God was watching, he liked lions, so God slid down from Heaven on a religious giraffe's neck to the ground. 'Who are you, sir?' said Lion. 'I am Mr God. If you don't believe me, ask Giraffe!'

Lion did, and Giraffe said, 'Oh yes, he's God.'

'There,' said God. 'If you still don't believe me, ask me a difficult question.'

'OK,' said Lion. 'How much is 2×2?'

'Four,' said God.

'Oh yes,' said Lion. 'You're God all right.'

'Good,' said God. 'Close your eyes and say "Miggle Moggle Cake".'

Lion did. When he opened his eyes God had gone back home. But Lion now had a lovely lovely mane of beautiful black hair, and he was so happy he married a Roman Catholic giraffe and lived happily ever after until the next day.

SPIKE MILLIGAN, *A Book of Milliganimals*

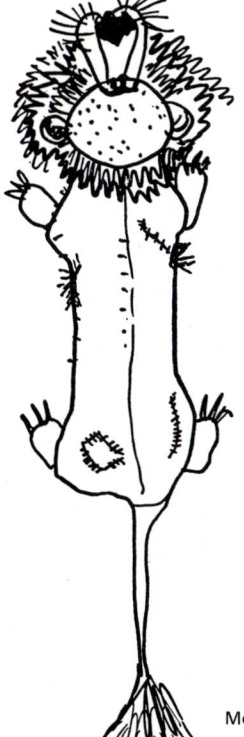

Monkey's view of Bald Twit Lion

Charles

The day Laurie started kindergarten he renounced corduroy overalls with bibs and began wearing blue jeans with a belt; I watched him go off the first morning with the older girl next door, seeing clearly that an era of my life was ended, my sweet-voiced nursery-school tot replaced by a long-trousered, swaggering character who forgot to stop at the corner and wave goodbye to me.

He came home the same way, the front door slamming open, his cap on the floor, and the voice suddenly became raucous shouting, 'Isn't anybody *here*?'

At lunch he spoke insolently to his father, spilled Jannie's milk, and remarked that his teacher said that we were not to take the name of the Lord in vain.

'How *was* school today?' I asked, elaborately casual.

'All right,' he said.

'Did you learn anything?' his father asked.

Laurie regarded his father coldly. 'I didn't learn nothing,' he said.

'Anything,' I said. 'Didn't learn anything.'

'The teacher spanked a boy, though,' Laurie said, addressing his bread and butter. 'For being fresh,' he added with his mouth full.

'What did he do?' I asked. 'Who was it?'

Laurie thought. 'It was Charles,' he said. 'He was fresh. The teacher spanked him and made him stand in a corner. He was awfully fresh.'

'What did he do?' I asked again, but Laurie slid off his chair, took a cookie, and left, while his father was still saying, 'See here, young man.'

The next day Laurie remarked at lunch, as soon as he sat down, 'Well, Charles was bad again today.' He grinned enormously and said, 'Today Charles hit the teacher.'

'Good heavens,' I said, mindful of the Lord's name, 'I suppose he got spanked again?'

'He sure did,' Laurie said. 'Look up,' he said to his father.

'What?' his father said, looking up.

'Look down,' Laurie said. 'Look at my thumb. Gee, you're dumb.' He began to laugh insanely.

'Why did Charles hit the teacher?' I asked quickly.

'Because she tried to make him colour with red crayons,' Laurie said. 'Charles wanted to colour with green crayons so he hit the teacher and she spanked him and said nobody play with Charles but everybody did.'

cheeky

biscuit

The third day – it was Wednesday of the first week – Charles bounced a seesaw onto the head of a little girl and made her bleed and the teacher made him stay inside all during recess. Thursday Charles had to stand in a corner during storytime because he kept pounding his feet on the floor. Friday Charles was deprived of blackboard privileges because he threw chalk.

On Saturday I remarked to my husband, 'Do you think kindergarten is too unsettling for Laurie? All this toughness and bad grammar, and this Charles boy sounds like such a bad influence.'

'It'll be all right,' my husband said reassuringly. 'Bound to be people like Charles in the world. Might as well meet them now as later.'

On Monday Laurie came home late, full of news. 'Charles,' he shouted as he came up the hill; I was waiting anxiously on the front steps, 'Charles,' Laurie yelled all the way up the hill, 'Charles was bad again.'

'Come right in,' I said, as soon as he came close enough. 'Lunch is waiting.'

'You know what Charles did?' he demanded, following me through the door. 'Charles yelled so in school they sent a boy in from first grade to tell the teacher she had to make Charles keep quiet, and so Charles had to stay after school. And so all the children stayed to watch him.'

'What did he do?' I asked.

'He just sat there,' Laurie said, climbing into his chair at the table. 'Hi Pop, y'old dust mop.'

'Charles had to stay after school today,' I told my husband. 'Everyone stayed with him.'

'What does this Charles look like?' my husband asked Laurie. 'What's his other name?'

'He's bigger than me,' Laurie said. 'And he doesn't have any rubbers and he doesn't ever wear a jacket.'

Monday night was the first Parent–Teachers meeting, and only the fact that Jannie had a cold kept me from going; I wanted passionately to meet Charles's mother. On Tuesday Laurie remarked suddenly, 'Our teacher had a friend come see her in school today.'

'Charles's mother?' my husband and I asked simultaneously.

'Naaah,' Laurie said scornfully. 'It was a man who came and made us do exercises. Look.' He climbed down from his chair and squatted down and touched his toes. 'Like this,' he said. He got solemnly back into his chair and said, picking up his fork, 'Charles didn't even *do* exercises.'

'That's fine,' I said heartily. 'Didn't Charles want to do exercises?'

121

'Naaah,' Laurie said. 'Charles was so fresh to the teacher's friend he wasn't *let* do exercises.'

'Fresh again?' I said.

'He kicked the teacher's friend,' Laurie said. 'The teacher's friend told Charles to touch his toes like I just did and Charles kicked him.'

'What are they going to do about Charles, do you suppose?' Laurie's father asked him.

Laurie shrugged elaborately. 'Throw him out of the school, I guess,' he said.

Wednesday and Thursday were routine; Charles yelled during story hour and hit a boy in the stomach and made him cry. On Friday Charles stayed after school again and so did all the other children.

With the third week of kindergarten Charles was an institution in our family; Jannie was being a Charles when she cried all afternoon; Laurie did a Charles when he filled his wagon full of mud and pulled it through the kitchen; even my husband, when he caught his elbow in the telephone cord and pulled telephone, ash tray, and a bowl of flowers off the table, said, after the first minute, 'Looks like Charles.'

During the third and fourth weeks there seemed to be a reformation in Charles; Laurie reported grimly at lunch on Thursday of the third week, 'Charles was so good today the teacher gave him an apple.'

'What?' I said, and my husband added warily, 'You mean Charles?'

'Charles,' Laurie said. 'He gave the crayons around and he picked up the books afterward and the teacher said he was her helper.'

'What happened?' I asked incredulously.

'He was her helper, that's all,' Laurie said, and shrugged.

'Can this be true, about Charles?' I asked my husband that night. 'Can something like this happen?'

'Wait and see,' my husband said cynically. 'When you've got a Charles to deal with, this may mean he's only plotting.'

He seemed to be wrong. For over a week Charles was the teacher's helper; each day he handed things out and he picked things up; no one had to stay after school.

'The PTA meeting's next week again,' I told my husband one evening. 'I'm going to find Charles's mother there.'

'Ask her what happened to Charles,' my husband said. 'I'd like to know.'

'I'd like to know myself,' I said.

On Friday of that week things were back to normal. 'You know what Charles did today?' Laurie demanded at the lunch table, in a voice slightly awed. 'He told a little girl to say a word and she said it and the teacher washed her mouth out with soap and Charles laughed.'

'What word?' his father asked unwisely, and Laurie said, 'I'll have to whisper it to you, it's so bad.' He got down off his chair and went around to his father. His father bent his head down and Laurie whispered joyfully. His father's eyes widened.

'Did Charles tell the little girl to say *that*?' he asked respectfully.

'She said it *twice*,' Laurie said. 'Charles told her to say it *twice*.'

'What happened to Charles?' my husband asked.

'Nothing,' Laurie said. 'He was passing out the crayons.'

Monday morning Charles abandoned the little girl and said the evil word himself three or four times, getting his mouth washed out with soap each time. He also threw chalk.

My husband came to the door with me that evening as I set out for the PTA meeting. 'Invite her over for a cup of tea after the meeting,' he said. 'I want to get a look at her.'

'If only she's there,' I said prayerfully.

'She'll be there,' my husband said. 'I don't see how they could hold a PTA meeting without Charles's mother.'

At the meeting I sat restlessly, scanning each comfortable matronly face, trying to determine which one hid the secret of Charles. None of them looked to me haggard enough. No one stood up in the meeting and apologized for the way her son had been acting. No one mentioned Charles.

After the meeting I identified and sought out Laurie's kindergarten teacher. She had a plate with a cup of tea and a piece of chocolate cake; I had a plate with a cup of tea and a piece of marshmallow cake. We manoeuvred up to one another cautiously and smiled.

'I've been so anxious to meet you,' I said. 'I'm Laurie's mother.'

'We're all so interested in Laurie,' she said.

'Well, he certainly likes kindergarten,' I said. 'He talks about it all the time.'

'We had a little trouble adjusting, the first week or so,' she said primly, 'but now he's a fine little helper. With lapses, of course.'

'Laurie usually adjusts very quickly,' I said. 'I suppose this time it's Charles's influence.'

'Charles?'

'Yes,' I said, laughing, 'you must have your hands full in that kindergarten, with Charles.'

'Charles?' she said. 'We don't have any Charles in the kindergarten.'

SHIRLEY JACKSON

The Linesman

Three men arrived yesterday with their van and equipment to repair the telephone lines leading to the house opposite. Two of the men stayed at work in the house. The third carried his ladder and set it up against the telegraph pole twenty-five yards from the house. He climbed the ladder and beyond it to the top of the pole where, with his feet resting on the iron rungs which are embedded at intervals in the sides of the pole, he began his work, his hands being made free after he had adjusted his safety harness. He was not likely to fall. I did not see him climb the pole. I looked from my window and saw him already working, twisting, arranging wires, screwing, unscrewing, leaning back from the pole, dependent upon his safety belt, trusting in it, seeming in a position of comfort and security.

I stared at him. I was reluctant to leave the window because I was so intent upon watching the linesman at work, and because I wanted to see him descend from the pole when his work was finished. People in the houses near the telegraph pole had drawn their curtains; they did not wish to be spied upon. He was in an excellent position for spying, with a clear view into the front rooms of half a dozen houses.

The clouds, curds and whey, were churned from south to north across the sky. It was one of the first Sundays of spring. Washing was blowing on the clothes lines in back gardens; youths were lying in attitudes of surrender beneath the dismantled bellies of scooters; women were sweeping the Saturday night refuse from their share of the pavement. Perhaps it was time for me to have something to eat — a cup of coffee, a biscuit, anything to occupy the ever marauding despair.

But still I could not leave my position at the window. I stared at the linesman until I had to screw up my eyes to avoid the bright stabs of spring light. I watched the work, the snipping, twisting, joining, screwing, unscrewing of bolts. And all the time I was afraid to leave the window. I kept my eyes fixed upon the linesman slung in his safety harness at the top of the telegraph pole.

You see, I was hoping that he might fall.

JANET FRAME

The Woollen Bank Forgeries

When I was nine years old I developed an insane passion for a cricket set on Woolworth's toy counter. This was in the days when everything at Woollie's cost either threepence or sixpence. Sixpence for the bat, ball sixpence, stumps sixpence, bails threepence, pads sixpence apiece, analysis book threepence, total three shillings. I made up my mind that I was going to have the cricket set. Long before I worked out how I was going to steal the money I was rehearsing what I would say to my mother when I took the gear home for the first time.

'No, only they've started a cricket team in our class. And do you know who's got to look after all the stuff, mam? Me.'

Immediate suspicion. 'How do you mean, you've got to look after it? Why can't they look after their own stuff?'

'Ah well, it's not really a school team, it's just our teacher. Old Webby. Mr Webb. He sees us all playing cricket in the street with an old tennis ball, so he says we could start our own team up in that field, and all look after the stuff in turns. He said we shouldn't be playing in the street.'

'Yes, and I've told you not to play in the street as well.'

My mother, with her flat damp voice, was so predictable that I could make up whole conversations with her before I got into the house, examining and re-examining each statement for flaws, leading myself up my own garden path and reconnoitring for trip-wires.

'Who paid out for it, then?'

'Mr Webb. He paid out for it himself.'

'What's *he* want to buy you cricket things for?' And so on.

First I had to get the money. I had several sources of income, but none large enough to get three shillings together at one go. The blue cup on the panshelf where she kept the pennies for the gas, that was worth twopence at one swoop, or perhaps threepence, depending on how full it was, but never more. Or the fish and chips: by buying twopennyworth instead of threepennyworth I could save a penny, but it was a risk. She always knew.

I thought for a long time that she had someone down there in the fish shop who ran back and told her what I'd bought.

'How many chips did you get?'

'Threepennorth.'

'How many chips did you get?'

'Threepennorth.'

'How – many – chips – did – you – get?'

'Told you, threepennorth.'

'You didn't get threepennorth at all. You got twopennorth. Didn't you?'

'No.'

'Didn't you?'

'No.'

'*Didn't* you?'

'Yes.'

'Where's that penny?'

'What penny?'

'I'll give you what penny, my lad! What have you done with it?'

'Lost it!'

'You didn't lose it at all. You've spent it! Have you spent it? You can't keep your hands off nothing, can you?'

I got sixpence a month from the church for singing in the choir, and threepence to take to the Wolf Cubs on Friday night towards the excursion to the Zoo. And sixpence on Monday morning to take to school and put in the bank. And twopence milk money, which I spent on myself as a matter of course.

Bank day was the big ceremony of the week. Each one of us at school had a little, green, linen-backed bank book, and on Monday mornings we paid in our sixpences or, in some rare cases, shillings and even half-crowns, to the Woollen Bank. The teacher acted as agent or collector for the bank. We started first thing, after the attendance register had been called. Webby would call out the names again, in a different order for some obscure reason, and this time we would march up in turn and pay out our money and have it entered in our little green books.

'Littlewood?'

'Here, sir.'

'Yes, we can see you're here, Littlewood. Where's your bank money?'

'Forgot it, sir.'

'You'd forget your head if it was loose, wouldn't you, Littlewood? All right. Patterson?'

'Sir.'

It cut very nicely into the geography class.

Some boys drew their money out regularly every four or five weeks, in florins and half-crowns, whenever their fathers were on short time; and some never had anything in the bank at all except an erratic sixpence on the wrong side of Christmas.

My own account usually went up to ten or twelve shillings before my mother made me draw it out to buy a pair of boots or something, and then we would start again at sixpence a week.

'Parker?'

'Sir.'

'Richards?'

'Drawing out, sir.'

'You're always drawing out, Richards.'

I had nothing in the bank. A neat red double line marked the last withdrawal and the new boots were squeaky on my feet. A sixpence screwed up in newspaper was ready to start the account again.

'Newbould.'

'Sir.'

'Well, move yourself, Newbould.'

'Haven't anything to put in, sir.'

'Why not?'

'My mother says we can't afford it this week, sir.'

'All right, Newbould. – Baker?'

'Sir.'

'Jordan?'

'Sir.'

I had sixpence in my pocket, wrapped up in a piece torn from the margin of the *Argus*. The first shiver ran down my back as I imagined dropping it in the playground and Webby recognizing it as bank money.

'It's what my mother gave me to get a cut loaf, sir.'

Five more like this would make three shillings. Twopence milk money would pay the tram fare to and from Woollie's.

'Here, why hasn't Mr Webb filled your bank book up?'

'Eh? Oh, he doesn't, sometimes. He sometimes leaves it till the end of the month.'

'Well, that's a funny way of doing it. How does he know how much you've paid in?'

'Ah, well, he's got a big book with it all written down.'

I never got the cricket set. On the way home from school, going the long way round while I worked out full and detailed dialogues with my mother about the bank book, I passed the Chocolate Cabin, the sweetshop belonging to the Regal cinema. In the little side window there was always a card advertising this or that assortment, and today there was a new card all about Ascot Royal, the new quarter-pound selection box. I went in and bought it, a box slightly smaller than the dummy in the window, and told them it was for my mother's birthday.

I ate the chocolates in quick bites all the way home. I never knew there were so many in a quarter of a pound. Even accounting for the bits of chocolate-coloured straw in three corners, I couldn't eat them all. I had five left when I approached our street. I put two in a privet hedge, gave one away to a little girl who was playing in her vest at the side of the road, and carried two home. I told my mother Mr Webb had given them to me.

'What's he want to give you chocolates for?'

'I don't know. He gave us all two each out of a big box.'

'He must have more money than sense.'

The sixpences slid slowly by. The second one I spent on my way to school on sugared almonds, which I had always fancied. The third one I kept until night and then went to the Regal and saw a film about a train in which the carriage door opens and someone throws a severed hand into the compartment.

I have dreamt about it since but I did not dream about it then, although I would lie awake wondering what was going to happen about the bank money. The fourth one I spent on an enormous wood-fibre scribbling block and told my mother that the rag and bone man was giving them away outside our school. The fifth sixpence was rolled away in pennies at a small and shoddy fair that halted for the day on some waste ground.

When I had got through two and sixpence my mother looked in the bank book. It was bound to happen sooner or later, and each Monday morning when she gave the book to me and each Monday dinnertime when I handed it back, another sixpence spent, I would jump small hurdles of apprehension, my eyes scouring her face for traces of suspicion and my ears strained to catch faint lilts of accusation in her voice.

It was, as a matter of fact, on a Wednesday. She had been going on about my wearing down the heels of my new boots and as usual she went on to drag up some other topic. My mother was too tired for spontaneous wrath. The graver sins were always hoarded until she could launch her rage with the touch-paper of some pettier misdemeanour.

'And another thing, why hasn't Mr Webb filled in your bank book?'

It suddenly seemed ridiculous that she had only now got round to asking about it.

'Eh? Oh, he doesn't, sometimes. He sometimes leaves it till the end of the month.'

'How do you mean, he leaves it to the end of the month? Of course he doesn't leave it to the end of the month.'

'Ah no, but he's started doing, because he's got 2B's books to do as well. So he like collects them and fills them in at the end of the month.'

E

'Have you been paying that money in?'

'Eh? Course I've been paying it in, what do you think I've been doing with it? He just marks it up every month, that's all.'

'Well, there's five weeks here not marked up. If I find out you've taken that money yourself . . .'

'Course I haven't taken it, what do I want with it?' I had rehearsed this too. I had rehearsed it, under the sweating blankets, every inch of the way to the reformatory. 'He just hasn't marked it up. He's got a big book and he puts it in that.'

'Well, he can just take it out again. Because I'm drawing it out. You can just get that money drawn out on Monday. Because I need it. And you can just tell him to mark that book in future.'

'I've told him. He doesn't take any notice.'

'He will take notice if I go down to that school.'

I prayed. Please God, get me out of this one and don't let her count the gas money on the panshelf, then I'll be all right.

It was a question of two and six. Better than letting it drag on until there was ten shillings to find, or twelve shillings. At the back of my mind I had already planned where the money was coming from. The Cub excursion to the Zoo was about eight weeks off. The full cost of the outing was five shillings, and there was three shillings so far in the kitty.

On Friday, while a game of British Bulldog was going on, I straightened my jersey and sought out Baloo at the back of the hall and told her I would not be going on the excursion.

'Why not?'

'My mother says we can't afford it.'

'But it's only threepence a week. Surely she can spare threepence a week?'

'No, it's not that, miss. She wants to draw out what we've put in already. To get a shirt.'

Baloo gave me her keen social worker's glance but I was not afraid of that.

''Cos I've only got one shirt and it's all torn.'

'Well, it's a shame. It's only another two shillings and you'd have enough to go on the trip.'

'I know. She says I can go another year.'

At the end of the evening, after Taps, Baloo put the three shillings in a clean envelope and handed it over. I kept it in my pocket and worried all night in case my mother went through my trousers and found it.

'What's this money?'

'Eh? Oh, it's what I drew out of the bank for you. Forgot to tell you, they always pay out on Fridays now.'

'Well you only had two and six in. What's this extra?'

'Interest.'

On Saturday morning I spent my last sixpence on toffee, reducing the sum to half a crown. On Saturday afternoon, when my mother was over at the cemetery I got out the blue ink and the red ink and got to work on the bank book.

It wasn't a bad forgery. First of all I added five sixpences together, copying five consecutive Mondays' dates from the doggy calendar by the mantelpiece. And then, carefully tracing an imitation of Webby's scrawl, I put 'Withdrn.—2s. 6d.'. Drew a double red line under it, as he did. Blotted it. Panicked, at the sudden realization that my mother might look at the bank book again before Monday. Prayed. Burned the blotting paper and disturbed the ash with the poker so that she could not fish it out and decipher what I had written.

At Monday dinnertime she got her half-crown and her bank book back. She glanced at the green book perfunctorily and put it away for ever. I had already decided to lose it down the fever drain if she ever opened that account again. I went out into the yard and stood on my hands against the lavatory door, for pleasure, and it was Friday, Club night, before the gnawing fears began again and I began to wonder what would happen if she ever ran into Baloo.

I spent the threepence she gave me for the Zoo excursion. I was having some very rich weeks. I had a feeling that when it came to it they might take me on the excursion for nothing, out of charity, and my only worry as the weeks passed was whether Baloo would call at the house and put this proposition to my mother.

'Just come in here. Now then. What have you done with all that money I gave you to give to Miss Dickinson?'

But when the last Friday came there was no question of it. They made their elaborate arrangements, to meet for the long trip at the Corn Exchange at seven in the morning with a packed dinner and a packed tea, and to go to the lavatory before they got on the coach.

I was up at six on Saturday morning and in my uniform, neckerchief straight, green garter tabs in position, by half-past. My last fear was that my mother would insist on taking me to the Corn Exchange. But she gave me my meals in a large brown paper bag, twopence for the tram fare and twopence for myself, and kissed me, I should think for the first time since I was in my pram. I went slowly up the empty street with sevenpence in my pocket –

fourpence from my mother and threepence the last instalment on the Zoo money – planning the long day and marvelling at the cold brightness of the workman's morning.

I went to the park where the gates were still locked, climbed the railings and had the lake to myself to walk round twenty times before the ranger appeared in the distance and I ran into the woods nearby where the ferns were still wet. I sat for a long time on a green bench and ate the first sandwich, cheese and onion, from my paper bag. I went from tree to tree, counting a hundred by each one before moving on. I nearly slept in the long grass. I took a piece of stone and tried to scrape my initials in the old men's shelter and then took fright and ran away again. The sandwiches were finished and I was down to the bun and apple.

At the top of the hill on the edge of the woods, at the far side of the park, I stopped at the ramshackle wooden shop and bought some liquorice bootlaces and a twopenny chocolate whirl. I sat on the long low wall by the side of the road and eventually a man came by and stopped and turned round and gave me the Wolf Cub salute. Shyly, without getting up, I put my own two fingers and saluted him back.

'I'm the Akela of the 23rd South-east Pack. What's your Pack?'

'Twenty-second North-east, sir.'

'And where are they?'

'They've gone off to Manchester for the day, sir, to the Zoo. Only my mother wouldn't let me go.'

He moved off and full of guilt I went back into the woods and walked around the trees while the day wore on.

When the sky was getting dark and I was tired, I set off home slowly, the longest way, sometimes walking backwards to waste the last half hour, and rehearsing what I would say to my mother. The street was empty again. My mother was in the kitchen, washing clothes and straining her eyes in the gloom to save the light. I flopped down on the buffet by the empty fire and waited for her to speak so that I could discover what she knew.

'Just look at you! Where've you been?'

'Zoo, where do you think I've been?'

'I'd have thought you'd been down the pit to look at you. You're black bright! Just look at your jersey.'

For the first time I examined my clothes, stained with grass and tree-bark, my boots streaked with white where the dew had dried on them, my hands and knees lined with rust where I had stood so long gripping the railings round the woods, remembering what I had read or seen at the Regal about zoos.

'Well, it's mucky, is the Zoo. We sat down on some grass for a picnic.'

'You look as though you've been sat down in a coal cellar.'

'Hey, mam, did you know elephants squirt water at each other when they have a bath?'

'You look as though *you* need a bath, never mind the elephants.'

'Well they do, they squirt each other. And we saw all these monkeys having a party.'

'Anyone'd think you were a monkey to look at you. And what's that tear in your trousers?'

I kept her talking, giving her opportunities to accuse me if she wanted to, but there was no more than routine disapproval in her voice. I told her about the zebras, the camel, the seals catching fish and the chimpanzee that stole a schoolboy's cap and ran away with it. She rubbed at my face and knees with a cold flannel caked in soap and listened to all I had to say. At the end she said:

'And who said you could give that tip-up lorry away to Jackie Hardcastle?'

'I didn't give it to him. I only lent it to him.'

'Well you can just stop lending things. And you get it back to-morrow morning. And don't you lend out things again.'

I went to bed and undressed in the dark. I slept and in the morning it was Sunday and I went to church. I still had three pennies left out of my sevenpence. I put them on the collection plate, for my criminal career was over. I was glad she had found out about the tip-up lorry, and for the first time in many months I had no fears at all. I was going to stop stealing the gas-money.

In the robing room, one of the other choirboys spoke to me.

'Hey, Newbouldy, where had you been yesterday afternoon in your Cub clothes?'

'When?'

'Yesterday, when do you think? You hadn't been on that Zoo excursion, I know that much, because they didn't come back till ten o'clock last night.'

'Where did you see me, then? On the golf-links?'

'No, in your street. You were just going home.'

I felt the low, watery thud at the bottom of my stomach. Struggling out of my surplice I said, 'What time was it?'

'Don't ask me, kid. 'Bout half past twelve. One o'clock. When it got right dark. Just before it started pelting down with rain.'

I ran all the way home, almost crying, and too seized with fear to rehearse any explanations about being sent home early from the Zoo by special coach. I had time to wonder why I hadn't thought to come down this way, past the church, and see the time by the old clock. Half-remembered snatches of the previous night's talking darted through my head, and it seemed now that her words had been larded with suspicion and disbelief, and that she was just waiting for some little incident to spark her off into the grand recrimination.

'Why did you tell me you'd been on that excursion?'

'What excursion?'

'I'll give you what excursion before I've finished, my lad.'

But in the house everything was quiet. She was making Yorkshire puddings and she even asked me if I would like to stir the batter, a great favour.

I tested her, deliberately talking about the zoo and giving her a chance to contradict me.

'Hey, the Scouts are going to that Zoo next month as well. Where we went to.'

'Never mind the Scouts, just watch what you're doing.'

'I bet their coach doesn't go as fast as ours. It didn't half go fast. We were there in no time.'

'Just watch what you're doing.'

I created the little incident, giving her an opening to get on to the bigger issues; I splashed batter over the clean newspapers that lined the kitchen table. But she only said: 'You're going to have that on the floor if you don't stop your chattering and watch what you're doing.'

I tested her and tested her for a week before I let the subject drop. And she never said anything. A fortnight later she met Baloo while she was out shopping and had a long talk with her. I tested her again about the Zoo. But she never said anything.

KEITH WATERHOUSE

Blackberry Motorist

The blackberry vines grew all around and climbed like green dragon tails the sides of some old abandoned warehouses in an industrial area that had seen its day. The vines were so huge that people laid planks across them like bridges to get at the good berries in the centre of them.

There were many bridges reaching into the vines. Some of them were five or six planks long and it took careful balancing to get back in there because if you fell off, there were nothing but blackberry vines for fifteen feet or so beneath you, and you could really hurt yourself on their thorns.

This was not a place you went casually to gather a few blackberries for a pie or to eat with some milk and sugar on them. You went there because you were getting blackberries for the winter's jam or to sell them because you needed more money than the price of a movie.

There were so many blackberries back in there that it was hard to believe. They were huge like black diamonds but it took a lot of mediaeval blackberry engineering, chopping entrances and laying bridges, to be successful like the siege of a castle.

'The castle has fallen!'

Sometimes when I got bores with picking

blackberries I used to look into the deep shadowy dungeon-like places way down in the vines. You could see things that you couldn't make out down there and shapes that seemed to change like phantoms.

Once I was so curious that I crouched down on the fifth plank of a bridge that I had put together way out there in the vines and stared hard into the depths where thorns were like the spikes on a wicked mace until my eyes got used to the darkness and I saw a Model A sedan directly underneath me.

I crouched on that plank for a long time staring down at the car until I noticed that my legs were cramped. It took me about two hours to tunnel my way with ripped clothes and many bleeding scratches into the front seat of that car with my hands on the steering wheel, a foot on the gas pedal, a foot on the brake, surrounded by the smell of castle-like upholstery and staring from twilight darkness through the wind-shield up into green sunny shadows.

Some other blackberry pickers came along and started picking blackberries on the planks above me. They were very excited. I think it was the first time they had ever been there and seen blackberries like that. I sat there in the car underneath them and listened to them talk.

'Hey, look at this blackberry!'

RICHARD BRAUTIGAN

Little Foxy's Bonfire Night

The dark night air felt full of smoke and roasted spuds. There were glares in the sky, from hundreds of bonfires all over Woodlestown. Fireworks banging and spluttering and fizzing. Oh boy. Soon be round our fire now. But first felt in my pocket for the tuppence which I'd saved up. Went to Mrs Taylor's corner shop for some bangers. Mrs Taylor's sold everything. Yo-yos, cabbages, fire-lights. Nice old lady, hair cut short, like a girl's, though really she was about a hundred and six. First knew her, a bit scared. Got to know her better when she came to our house on Sunday nights, tell our fortunes with tea-leaves in a cup. Spoke in a soft voice, always smiling. Clever though. Could perform magic with the spirits. Sometimes when she came to our house, we had a meeting. All sat round a card table. Me, Grannie Fox, Mrs Thingy and one or two other women. Sat round the table, lights out, hands spread out on it, fingers touching. Then, when everything's ready, Mrs Taylor asked the table questions.

'Are the spirits with us yet? Knock once for yes, and twice for no.'

Table rocked one of its legs, bangs either once or twice, depending on whether the spirits are with us yet or not. Sometimes takes them about ten minutes to come. When they do come, nobody knows except Mrs Taylor. Asks more questions. Like, will my dad be going on a long journey? Never asked questions like, what's it like when you're dead? Or, who'll get the cane at school tomorrow? Still, she was all right when you got to know her. Nothing to be scared of, like. Well, not much.

Went in for the bangers. Nobody about.

'SHOP.'

Shouted, loud as I could.

'SHOP.'

Nothing happened for a while. All very quiet. Imagined she must be talking to the spirits. Waited, looked at all the rows of bottles of sweets, counter shelves. Striped humbugs, like Bumper Flanagan used to buy, lozenges, fruit drops, pastilles.

Then by heck!

Nearly jumped out of my skin.

Mrs Taylor suddenly appeared from right behind where I was looking. As though she'd come out of one of the big bottles of humbugs, back row.

'Now then, luv. What do you want?'

'You made me jump. Four ha'penny bangers please.'

Got a big coloured box, under the counter. Asked me which kind

I wanted. Picked one Little Demon, two Flashes, and one Cannon. Then Mrs Taylor picked up a Whizzbang.

'Here you are, I'll buy this one for you.'

Good old Mrs Taylor.

'Does Grannie Fox know you've come out?'

'Yes.'

Looked at me carefully. Hoped she wouldn't go across to our house, spill the beans about seeing me. Out of the shop, round by the cobbler's. Could hear the fire crackling already. Began to run. Turned the corner, into Big Buzz's street. And there it was.

What a fire!

Blaze blinded, man. Burning away like Joe Chuff.

Crackling, spluttering, sparks flying about all over the place. Lighting up houses, both sides of the street, as though it was a searchlight. So hot, had to shield my eyes with my hand, see what was happening. Soon got used to the glare. Could see all the gang, standing about with bloodshot eyes, dirty faces. Letting off fireworks. Jumping about.

'Yippee! Yippee!'

Then Big Buzz spotted me.

'Hey, Little Foxy. Where've you been?'

Came over told him what had happened.

'Will you get your ass tanned then?'

He sounded very serious.

'Suppose so. But it doesn't matter. I've hidden the strap.'

Big Buzz laughed. Told the others. They laughed. Thought, it's all right them lot laughing. They're all right. But what about me? Anyway. There's nothing to worry about, yet, I hope. Then Jibs came up to me. Eating peas, out of a saucer.

'Where did you get them, man?'

'Ommmmmm-upppum-ummmmmmmm dishing 'em out.'

Spoke with his mouth full. Could hardly understand a word.

'You what. What did you say?'

Jibs looked at me. Cleared his mouth. Swallowing in big lumps. Then: 'Old Ma Morton's dishing them out. Go and get some, man. Quick. Before they're all done.'

Nipped off, over to Ma Morton's doorway. Had a big pan of peas, boiling on a gas ring. Talking away to three other women, all talking as well. Just stood there. Waited till she saw me. Then she shouted:

'Do you want some peas, lad. Well go and get yer-sen a saucer off of somebody who's finished. Then bring it to me, luv. I'll see you get some, then.'

Went off. Found Jibs. Waited till he'd finished eating. Borrowed his saucer and spoon. Ma Morton gave me a big dollop of peas without washing the saucer. Didn't worry me. Knew Jibs all right. Been to their house for tea. Like he'd been to ours once. Put loads of salt and vinegar on this dollop of peas. Asked Ma Morton for some pepper. Looked, laughed, shouted:

'Fussy ha'porths, you lads, aren't you?'

She went into the house. Wished I hadn't asked. Getting the peas for nothing, to start with. Soon she came back with some pepper.

'There you are, at your service.'

Put plenty on my peas. Mixed everything up with the spoon. They were them lovely mushy peas, like you get at Woodlestown Feast.

'You'll have to tell Grannie Fox how to make peas like this.'

This made Ma Morton laugh.

'Ha-ha. Yes, I will. Ha-ha.'

Finished them off in no time. Went to find Jibs, let my bangers off with him. Over at the other side of the fire. He was with Big Buzz and the others. Big Buzz had got his dander up. Letting off steam about Jibs's dad and Willie J, throwing lumps on the fire.

'Cor-luvva me. They've only just flipping come. There they are.

collected objects for the bonfire

Throwing all our blinking chumps on. Who do they think they are, Laurel and Hardy? They never did any chumping with us.'

Then Al Toddy chimed in.

'No, did they 'ellerslike. Come on.'

They both marched over, had a big argument with Jibs's dad and Willie J. Jibs turned to me:

'Aw, come on. Nowt to do with us. Let's go and let your bangers off.'

Walked round the fire until we found the right-sized stick. Shoved it in one end of the fire. It was that hot, nearly scorched your eyebrows off. Then chose the Little Demon. Took the stick out of the fire.

'By the Jeebus, it's bluddy hot.'

End of the stick was in flames. Waited until it died down and went red. Lit the banger's blue fuse paper. It began to fizz. Jibs got excited.

'Quick, man. Throw it. Before it goes off in your hand.'

Waited another second or two. Then. Threw it, high as I could. It went up to about the top of Ma Morton's bedroom window. Then it went off.

WHAM!

Like a pistol shot.

'YAROUSH!'

Me and Jibs let out a big yell. Kidded-on to be shot. Grabbed our stomachs. Staggered around like gangsters on the flicks when the cops have shot 'em down.

'You've got me. You've got me.'

Shouted out. Finished up rolling on the floor, in agony.

Used up all the bangers, then Ernie Tot saw us. Came over.

'How do, Ernie.'

'Hello, my boys. Hello.'

'Have the Gill Gang been to raid us yet?'

'The Gill Gang. No. No. Don't worry about them, my boy. I say, have you heard this joke?'

'No.'

'What's it about?'

'It's about an Englishman, Irishman, Scotsman and Jew, well, they all climbed this very tall haystack. But when they got on top, somebody took the ladder away and they couldn't get down. So the Englishman said, 'I shall jump down.' So he jumped and broke his leg. Then the Irishman jumped and he broke his arm. Then the Scotsman jumped, and he broke his collar-bone. But then the Jew got down safe and sound. Do you know how he did it?'

'No.'

'No.'

'Ha-ha. He greased his arse and slid down the rainbow.'

Took a second. Then.

'Ha-ha. Ha-ha, ha-ha.'

'That was good, wannit?'

'Ha-ha, ha-ha, ha-ha.'

Couldn't stop laughing for ages. Then saw Big Buzz, the others all talking, excited. Ernie Tot went over to investigate. Me and Jibs followed him. Then he came back to us, after he'd listened in.

'What's up?'

'I say, Al Toddy has dared Big Buzz to shove a jumping cracker under Old Ma Morton's chair.'

By heck!

'So watch out, man.'

Ma Morton sat the other side of the fire. On an old armchair. small stream With the springs busting out. One that we'd found in the beck. Going to sit the Guy Fawkes on it, burn it, later on. Big Buzz picked a Jumping Jim from Al Toddy's collection. All the gang went very quiet. Watched him move nearer the chair. He stopped, to light the Jumping Jim. Lit it. Waited a few seconds. Nipped round the back of the chair. Pushed the cracker underneath. Ma

Morton, so busy chatting, never noticed a thing. Big Buzz ran back to the rest of us. We watched, waited. Nothing happened. For ages and ages, it seemed. Wondered whether it was a dud. Or maybe the fuse had gone out?

And then, suddenly:

Fizz-fizz-fizz.

The Jumping Jim came flying out from under the chair. Banged away like merry-hell. Right underneath her legs. She yelled out, jumped up in the air, holding her frock, dancing around, could see all her bloomers, red ones. Looked like Auntie Bertha at the Swinging Cat, doing 'Can-Can' at a party on a Saturday night. Everybody laughed like heck. Then Ma Morton spotted us. Knew what had happened straight-away. Shook her mighty fists at us.

'Yer little devils. You'll have me in my grave, before you've done.'

Other women crowded round her. Good job it was Ma Morton that it happened to. Some of the others would have brought the coppers.

Forgotten all about Grannie Fox. Was having a right good time. Then saw Little Midge Madge with a bunch of other lasses. Letting off sparklers. Had her grey stockings on, up to her knees. And her navy-blue mac, belt tied round. Watched her for a few minutes. Wondered whether to go and talk to her. Then saw her mam. Keeping guard of them all. So I thought I'd better not.

Then I got a right shock.

Grannie Fox, red coat, scarf round her head, had just come round the corner. Began looking round. Heck, I thought, she would come just now. Hadn't seen me yet. Kidded on not to see her either. Went over, talk to Jibs. Short while, Ernie Tot came up to me.

'Hey, I say, Little Foxy. Your Grannie wants to see you.'

'I know. But I'm not going.'

'Now, now, my boy. Use your common sense. It will only be the worse for you if you don't go.'

Didn't say anything for a while. Just stood thinking. Then Jibs spoke up.

'Look, man. Tell you what to do. Go over to see her, else she'll only be getting more mad, and then I'll go and get Big Buzz to chat her up a bit.'

Didn't sound like a bad idea. Big Buzz could talk the hind leg off a donkey.

'All right, Jibs.'

Shoved my hands in my pockets. Looked miserable. Walked over to see Grannie Fox. Got up to her, thought, right, now for it. Probably get a belt round the ear, start with.

143

Saw me, snapped.

'So there you are.'

Mad as our house, she sounded.

'I knew I'd find you here. Thought I told you not to come. Well, you can just go . . .'

She was interrupted:

'Here you are, how do, Grannie Fox. Er . . . here, just in time for a plate of lovely peas. . . .'

It was Big Buzz, come to do his stuff. Good lad Jibs for telling him. Big Buzz shoved the peas into Grannie Fox's hands. Wondered whether she might give him a clout. But Big Buzz didn't give her time to think. Went on chatting her up.

'. . . I'm right glad you let him come, Grannie Fox. After all that chumping he's done with us. Would have been a right shame if he'd had to stay in. Lovely peas, aren't they? Would you like some more? What about some home-made treacle toffee? Or a bit of parkin, then? And how are you keeping these days. . . .'

gingerbread

Big Buzz gave me the nod. Slipped away. Quick as I could. Found Jibs. Told him what had happened.

'He can do anything, Big Buzz can, man. Anything at all. Told you everything would be all right. Just leave it to Big Buzz.'

Then Big Buzz came up to us. Told me that Grannie Fox said I could stay another half-hour. Then I'd have to be off home.

'And mek sure you go, an' all. Else Grannie Fox will have my ass for aniseed balls.'

'All right then.'

'Don't forget. Promised her you'd be home in half-an-hour.'

'Yer. All right.'

Thought, it's about time they made Big Buzz the King of England.

Stood around watching the fire get smaller. Then Big Buzz said it was time to burn the Guy. Tim and Al Toddy shoved the big chair on to the fire. Then Big Buzz sat the Guy in it. We all watched as the flames began to lick round his sides. His sacking trousers caught hold first, then the paint began to run off his face. Soon he had no hair, no eyes, no nose, no mouth. Looked very sad and frightened. Then the blaze licked his chops and in another few seconds began to blaze merrily. It brightened us all up again. Ernie Tot laughed.

'Ha-ha. I say. I wish it was Bonfire Night every night. We'd all have a . . .'

Didn't get time to finish. Gang of kids came charging round the corner. Threw bangers about all over the place, to scare everybody. Women screaming, kids shouting. Big Buzz and Al Toddy fighting like hell, stop these kids pinching the rest of the chumps. There was a right mix-up. Me and Jibs rugby-tackled this big kid who was trying to get at Big Buzz from behind. Then we were in the middle of hundreds of kids' legs and boots. It was worse than a rugby scrum, collapsed.

Then, suddenly, it was all clear. The gang of raiders charged off.

'It's bluddy Gill Gang getting their own back.'

'Yer. But they didn't get any chumps.'

'No. And a good job for them an' all.'

Heard somebody crying out. In pain.

'Oh, oh, oh.'

Looked round. Saw Ernie Tot holding his hand over one eye.

'One of them kids. Threw a firework in his face.'

Poor old Ernie Tot. He was going mad with the pain. Then Old Ma Morton came up to him. Made him take his hand away, while she had a look at his eye.

'Oh, my God.'

She cried out, turning her head away.

'Oh, my God. Somebody send for Doctor Senior straight away.'

Put her big arm round his shoulders, led Ernie away to her house. Another woman went to fetch Doctor Senior, taking Al Toddy with her for protection. Jibs was nearly crying himself.

'Poor old Ernie Tot. I bet it's blown his eye right out of its socket.'

'Yes. The dirty rats.'

Then Big Buzz shouted across to me.

'Hey, Little Foxy. Time you were off home.'

'Yer, all right. Just going.'

Watched the fire, dying down now, a few minutes longer. Then I went home. Wondered what Grannie Fox would be like when I got in.

NORMAN SMITHSON

Jackie the Jibber

It was him that give me my name, our barber: Jack the Jibber. Jibber? Well, it means jibbing in, don't it? Getting in places without paying. I can't remember the last time I ever paid to see anything; football, boxing, dog racing, there's nearly always a way, but of course it's boxing that's my speciality.

Me old man, he's a porter up the market at Covent Garden like I am, he's dead proud of me, he says, 'He's done the impossible, Jack has,' and it's true, really. I mean, I've jibbed in at places you wouldn't think you could *dynamite* your way in, not without a ticket, and never been caught: not once.

Anyway, like I was saying, the barber – he give me the name, after something I done at Earl's Court. It was the night Jim Pacey was fighting the American, Douglas, for the welterweight title and you couldn't move for police, there was two cordons of them, right the way round the stadium. I'm standing outside the main entrance and wondering how I'll get through when just at that moment the barber comes along.

He says, 'How's it going, Jack?' and I says, 'At the moment, it's very, very poor: but I'll be in.'

Well, the police weren't too bad, there's a way of dealing with police, you just got to show you ain't afraid of them, because that's when they get on top of you. I said, 'Will you kindly let me through, officer, I'm one of the seconds?' and at the next cordon, I done it again, but I still had to get past the commissionaire, and that wasn't going to be so easy. He's standing there at the turnstile, the one I've picked out, a big bloke with a red face, wearing the old uniform – they're all ex-Army, pigs, most of them – and I says, 'I'm Andy Cumming's brother' – that's one of the fighters – 'he's got me ticket for me, inside.'

The bloke says, 'I don't care who you are, you can't come inside without no ticket.' So I go on arguing with him, and in the end I make as if I'm going to climb over the turnstile and he gives me a push, which is what I been wanting him to do. So I comes down right on the turnstile and I says, 'Oh! Oh! You've dis-colated me knee! I'm going to sue the company!'

Well, that worries him properly, he changes his tune, then, he says, 'I'm very, very sorry, boy; here, you'd better come through,' And you know what the end of it was? I got down ringside and I finished up sitting in the barber's seat, that he'd paid three guineas for.

Looking at me, you wouldn't think I done all these things, because I mean, in appearance, I'm just an ordinary London boy, nothing to look at. But this is a help, I always reckon, because if you don't look like nothing in particular, then it's easier to disappear. Of course, you got to have a bit of style, as well, you got to be able to turn it on, like, now and again.

There was this time I was up at Manchester, at Belle Vue, Dave Kelly was fighting for the British title, light heavyweight, and where he goes, I go. He's my favourite, Dave, he's a marvellous fighter, I jibbed in all over the country to see him, Wembley, Harringay, Manchester, Leicester. I even went up as far as Glasgow, I jibbed the train ride, and all.

Anyway, Belle Vue, it's usually dead easy in the North, because up there, they don't really know, it's not like London. Only I had Ted Williams with me, this mate of mine, and I got through all right, but the commissionaire stops him. He says, 'Where's your ticket, then?' Ted was well embarrassed, he was well embarrassed. But I just turned round and said, 'He's with *me*, my man.'

Dave won that night, he took the title. He's got a big heart, that's what I like about him. A lovely left hand, too, I'm not denying that, but what I like about him is his heart; he'll never lie down, Dave won't. I seen him go on with a cut eye, a really bad one, the blood was pouring down his face, when even his corner wanted him to pack it in, but he went on, and in the end he stopped the other fellow, by my life, he stopped him in the thirteenth round.

But you got to think quickly, jibbing. Like this other time Dave was fighting at Harringay, against this American, Joey Harper, and the bloke stops me and asks for me ticket, just as I'm walking through. Well, I'm fumbling around, trying to think of something, when this other bloke comes along and he stops him, too, and he says, 'What about *your* ticket?' and he says 'I already shown it to you,' and I says, 'That's what I done, isn't it?'

Soon as Dave come into the ring that night, I was there, just like I always was: 'Hallo, Dave, all right, then, Dave?' and he'd be looking for me, he'd give me a smile, because I think he reckoned I brought him luck. I even been up in his corner, once, the night he defended his British title at Wembley against Lennie Haynes, I got a photo and all, to prove it – holding up his robe, for him to put on. One of the attendants tapped me on the shoulder and he says, 'What do you think *you're* doing there?' and I looks at him and I says, '*Do* you mind?' I says, 'I'm only the bloke that's holding the champion's robe, that's all,' and he apologized.

Me father used to get worried at times, he'd say, 'You got to watch it, Jack, they got more ways of killing the cat than drowning it, that lot has,' and I knew what he meant, but that added to it, if you see what I mean; knowing they'd probably sort me out if they got hold of me.

They done it with this other jibber, this Morrie Bass from out Edmonton way, that used to jib the Cup Final at Wembley Stadium. Year after year he'd be there, out on the field with the winning team, always in the photos. Then one year they come after him and grabbed him, and the police got stuck into him somewhere under the stand; there was half-a-dozen of them, he told me.

But I said to me father. 'Don't you worry, Dad, they won't catch Jack, I got a trick or two up me sleeve.'

Because this other fellow, he was asking for it; I mean, running out on the field every year in front of a hundred thousand people, and the Queen and all.

It was when I give this interview to the journalists that it all started, though, it started getting difficult. Afterwards, I was sorry I done it. I don't know how he even got on to it, somebody must of told him, but anyway he come over to me one night between fights at Shoreditch, when I was sitting ringside – I'd slipped into one of the Press boys' seats – and he said, 'You're Jackie the Jibber, ain't you?' I says, 'I don't know what you're talking about, I'm from the *Hackney Telegraph*,' it was the first name that come into me head, but he says, 'That's all right, Jack, I won't give you away, son, I heard a lot about you, that's all, I'd like to write an article on you. Come off and have a drink with me afterwards, eh, and we'll have a little talk about it.'

So I went with him and we had a few drinks, in fact I reckon I must have had a few too many because in the end he quoted me saying things I wasn't entitled to have said, like I was too clever for the lot of them, they'd never caught me and they never would, and the day I paid for a ticket to get in a boxing match, that'd be the day an English heavyweight would win the world title.

It all come out in the paper next day, one of the evening papers, it was, Jackie the Jibber, the bloke they couldn't catch, the Houdini of boxing. The old man said, 'Ay, ay; you didn't ought to have done that, son, you've challenged them, they'll be after you, now,' and I said, 'Well, they ain't got me picture, they don't know what I *look* like,' and he said, 'No, but they'll be looking for you.'

In fact the very next day in that paper they had an interview with the promoter of the fight, with Sam Dyment, who I'd never liked what I'd seen of him, saying, if Jackie does that again at one of my shows, he'll be in for trouble, I'm warning him. In fact what annoyed me was where he said he didn't believe I'd done it at all. He said, '*No*body can get into my shows without no ticket.' He said, 'Maybe he pinched somebody's seat that he wasn't entitled to, that I'm not denying, but he must have had a ticket of some sort.'

I wasn't going to stand for that, and I rang up this Bill Douglas, this journalist, and I said, 'Is that what he told you, this Dyment?' and he says, 'Yes, Jack, every word of it.'

I said, 'He's taking a diabolical liberty. When's his next show, then?' and he said, 'It's at Wembley again, November 10.'

'All right,' I says, 'I'll come up and I'll speak to you before the beginning of the main event, is that okay? You watch for me. And the next day you can put it in your paper that you seen me there, and that I didn't have no ticket. By my life; you can search me.'

Because I couldn't let him beat me, see, this Dyment. If I'd of let him beat me, I couldn't of showed me face no more, I'd of been ashamed of meself. Because this was who I was, Jackie the Jibber, everybody knew me, everyone up the market, everyone round where we lived, in Southwark, and if I'd've packed up now, that would of been the end of it.

When I got to Wembley, the night he had his next show on, it didn't seem no different than usual at first, I couldn't see no extra commissionaires or nothing. The only thing was, getting nearer, they seemed to be taking much longer, looking at the tickets. Then, hanging around in the background, I saw a couple of big blokes what I recognized, they'd been heavyweights, the pair of them, neither of them any good, but now I'd heard they was working for Dyment, round his office.

Well, I went straight up to one of the entrances, I put me hand in me pocket, then I made this face, like I'd just had a terrible shock. Then I went through all the other pockets one by one, pulling out everything that was in 'em and looking through it, and the commissionaire said, 'What's the matter, mate, lost your ticket?' and I said, 'No, wait a minute, it's got to be there, I remember picking it up off the mantelpiece at home, before I come out, I know I did,' and he says, 'Maybe you got your pocket picked; you come by tube?'

So I went on looking till he said, 'Remember the number, do you?' and I pretend to think about it, then I says, 'Yes, I believe I do, I wrote it down somewhere.' Then I look at the back of an envelope and I says, 'Here it is, Block Y, Row J, Seat 23.'

'Well,' he says, 'It's lucky you done that, because we're very hot on tickets tonight, but as it is, you may get in. I'll let you through to see the box office manager, maybe you can sort it out with him.' He calls one of the other geysers over and he says, 'You take him,' then he lets me through, into this entrance hall they've got, and we goes through the door into the sort of passageway that runs right round the whole arena. The bloke says, 'Follow me,' and one moment I'm following him and the next he looks round and I've gone. In all that crowd, it was easy.

151

I found a good seat and all, I only had to change it the once, when the fellow come up and claims it, and before the big fight started, I went up and had a word with Bill Douglas, like I said I would. Next day he had it in his paper.

I rang him up the morning after that and says, 'Have you spoke to Dyment yet? What did he say?' and he says, 'He nearly went up the wall, he's really looking for you now. He said, "All right, I'll see to him, I'll get him sooner or later, it's just a matter of time, that's all." '

'Well,' I says, 'wish him the best of luck from me, then, will you?'

Me father was on at me again to give up, he says, 'What do you want to go on now for, Jack, you've proved it, ain't you? You've made a mug of him.'

I said, 'Yeah, but if I give up now, he'll think he's frightened me,' I said. 'I want to show him up proper; just once more, then I'll relin-guish me title.'

About a week or so after that, I opened me paper one morning and I said to meself, 'Here's me chance.' Dyment had signed up Dave Kelly for a world title fight, and he was going to put it on in the open air, at the White City.

I said to me father, 'This is it, this is what I been waiting for. I'll have me picture took shaking hands with the champ, because that's what he'll be, Dave, after the fight, he will *be* the new champion. Then I'll relin-guish me title, like I promised.'

Well, I made me plans, I had plenty of time, and when it come to the day before the fight I rang up Dyment. They didn't want to put me through at first but I said, 'You let me speak to him, it's to do with tomorrow's fight, it's a matter of life and death,' and in the end, they did.

I said, 'Mr Dyment?' and he said, 'Who's that?' and I says, 'Jackie,' and he says, 'Jackie who?' and I says, 'Jackie the Jibber, of course! I'll be there tomorrow, I just rung up to tell you so. I'll see you at the fight,' then I hung up, I was killing meself. Because I'd never had no time for him, not even before all this happened, going around with his big cigar and his smile, I'd never trusted him.

A boy could go in the ring and get his brains bashed out and that'd be the end of him, and the next promotion, Dyment would still be there, he'd still be smoking his cigar and talking about how modern kids hadn't got no guts, they wouldn't go in the ring no more; I'd like to of seen *him* there. But this thing with me, this put the lid on it. I thought, you got everything and I got nothing, and the little bit I *have* got, you want to take it away from me. I thought, what *difference* does it make to you whether I jib in or whether I don't, for the few shillings you'd get off of me if I *did* buy a ticket.

It's because you want to run everything, that's why, you want to control the lot, and as far as I'm concerned, I ain't going to be controlled.

Then I rung up Douglas at his newspaper and I said, 'You got a cameraman there tomorrow, and all?' and he says, 'Yes, we got one ringside,' and I says, 'You tell him to look out for me, tell him to look out for Jack at the end of the fight, in the champion's corner. That'll be Dave,' I said, 'he'll be the new champion.' I said, 'And this is me last appearance, I'm retiring after this, you tell your bloke to take the picture. I've told Dyment I'll be there.'

He put it in the paper, too, *Jackie the Jibber's Last Appearance*.

I got there early that night, there was a big crowd, they expected sixty thousand. I hung about in the official car park till this big Rolls Royce arrived and out got this Lord, the Steward of the Board of Boxing Control, all dressed up in a dinner jacket and a black bow tie, and his wife all dressed in furs, and I followed them up to the visitors' entrance, straight through past the commissionaire, that said, 'Good evening, sir,' then when Dyment come forward to shake hands with him, Lord Whatsisname, I done me disappearing act. There was nothing to it, because I was wearing it too, the old black tie and dinner jacket, I'd hired them.

It's amazing the difference it makes, really, the way they treat you, stewards and commissionaires and all.

I come up to the ring before the big fight, the title fight, and I called good luck to Dave, and he looked surprised at first and I said, 'What's the matter, then, don't you recognize me now I'm dressed proper?' then he did recognize me, and he smiled.

He won it beautiful, of course, he had the fellow down three times in the eighth, lovely left hand punching, and the fellow couldn't hurt him. When it was over, I fought me way through the crowd, then I got through the police and the attendants, I was saying, 'Board of Control, Board of Control.' Then I got up in the ring and I shook hands with Dave, I said, 'Well done, Dave, well done, boy,' and the photographers was popping their bulbs all round us. Then up come Dyment to shake hands with him as well, still with the big cigar, and when he done it I said, 'Congratulations, Mr Dyment,' and I shook hands with him meself, I must have held it nearly a minute, for the photographers, and he was looking at me like he knew me, but he wasn't sure.

Then I said, 'That's *two* champions you just shook hands with, Mr Dyment,' and I jumped down from the ring and I was away. Not too quick, though, I mean, I was wearing me dinner jacket, wasn't I?

BRIAN GLANVILLE

Pantomime poem

'HE'S BEHIND YER!'
chorused the children
but the warning came too late.

The monster leaped forward
and fastening its teeth into his neck,
tore off the head.

The body fell to the floor
'MORE' cried the children
'MORE, MORE, **MORE**

MOR

MORE

MO

MO

Acknowledgements

For permission to use copyright material acknowledgement is made to the following:

Stories   For 'Simon Rodia, Architect and Builder of the Watts Towers' to the Committee for Simon Rodia's Towers in Watts; for 'A Table is a Table' and 'The Man Who Didn't Want to Know Any More' by Peter Bichsel translated by Michael Hamburger from *Stories For Children* to Calder & Boyars Ltd and Delacorte Press; for 'Blackberry Motorist' by Richard Brautigan from *Revenge of the Lawn* to Jonathan Cape Ltd and Simon Schuster Inc.; for 'The Boy Who Left Home to Learn Fear' by The Brothers Grimm translated by Heiner Bastian to Petersburg Press Ltd; for the extracts from *Tales of the Hodja* by Charles Downing to Oxford University Press and Henry Z. Walck Inc.; for 'Spoil the Child' by Howard Fast to The Curtis Publishing Co.; for 'The Linesman' by Janet Frame from *The Reservoir and Other Stories* to W. H. Allen Ltd; for 'Jackie the Jibber' by Brian Glanville to the author; for 'Charles' by Shirley Jackson from *The Lottery and Other Stories* to Michael Joseph and Farrar, Straus & Giroux Inc.; for 'Kamik' by Markoosie from *Harpoon of the Hunter* to McGill-Queen's University Press; for 'Pantomime Poem' by Roger McGough from *After the Merrymaking* to Jonathan Cape Ltd; for 'The Bald Twit Lion' by Spike Milligan from *A Book of Milliganimals* to Dennis Dobson; for 'Sport: The Kill' by Liam O'Flaherty from *Selected Short Stories of Liam O'Flaherty* to Jonathan Cape Ltd and The Devin-Adair Company; for the extract from *The World of Little Foxy* by Norman Smithson to Victor Gollancz Ltd; for 'The Animal That Drank Up Sound' by William E. Stafford from *The Rescue Year* to Harper & Row Inc.; for 'The Colt' by Wallace Stegner from *The Big Rock Candy Mountain* to Doubleday and Co. Inc. and Brandt & Brandt; for 'The Glass in the Field' by James Thurber from *Fables of Our Time* to Helen Thurber and Hamish Hamilton; for 'The Castaways' by Roland Topor translated by Margaret Crosland and David Le Vay from *Stories and Drawings* to Peter Owen Ltd; for 'Summat Queer on Batch' from *Folktales of England* to the University of Chicago Press; for 'Unexpected Good Fortune' traditional from *Fair Tale Tree* to the Hamlyn Publishing Group Ltd; for 'The Harpooning' by Ted Walker from *The Night Bathers* to Jonathan Cape Ltd; for 'The Woodwose' by Jill Paton Walsh from *Wordhoard* to Macmillan and Farrar, Straus & Giroux Inc.; for 'The Woollen Bank Forgeries' by Keith Waterhouse to the author; for 'Girlie Christian's Missing Leg' extract from an interview with Alan Whicker to Yorkshire Television Ltd; for 'The Dog With a Million Fleas' by Stuart Albert Widdows to the author and the Daily Mirror Children's Literary Competition.

Pictures   For the picture on pages 2–3 to Geoffrey Drury; pages 6–7 to Paul Almasy; pages 10–11 to Gunnar Forsell; pages 12–22 from *The Boy Who Left Home to Learn Fear*, Grimms Fairy Tales to David Hockney and Petersburg Press Ltd; pages 24–5 to Kingston Local History Museum;

page 26 to Madame Magritte and the Arts Council, London; page 28 to Library of Congress; page 29 to Jacques Henri Lartique, The John Hillelson Agency; pages 30–31 to Madame Magritte, Private Collection, Yorktown, New York, page 35 to Madame Magritte, Tate Gallery, London; page 44 to *Los Angeles Times*; pages 46–7 to Geoffrey Summerfield and Julius Shulman; page 50 to Institute of Archaeology, Oxford; pages 62–3 to National Maritime Museum, Greenwich; pages 74–5 to John Glashan; pages 78–9 to The John Hillelson Agency; photos Bert Hardy; page 88 to Dover Publications; pages 90–91 to Syndication International; pages 94–5 to The National Archives, New York; pages 106–7 to The John Hillelson Agency: photos Elliott Erwitt; page 110 to Prado, Madrid; pages 112–19 from *A Book of Milliganimals* by Spike Milligan, to the Artist and Dobson Books; pages 124–5 to Keystone Press; page 135 to James Lloyd; page 138 to Lucy Huws; pages 146–7 to *Sports Illustrated*: photo by Neil Leifer: Time Inc.

List of Illustrations

Index of Authors and Translators